The Amish of Canada

The Amish of Canada

Orland Gingerich

HERALD PRESS
Kitchener, Ontario
Scottdale, Pennsylvania

This book was originally published in 1972 by Conrad Press, Waterloo, Ontario.

THE AMISH OF CANADA

Published by Herald Press, Kitchener, Ont. N2G 4M5
Released simultaneously in the United States by
Herald Press, Scottdale, Pa. 15683
Library of Congress Catalog Card Number: 72-94800
International Standard Book Number: 0-8361-1856-1
Illustration by Douglas Ratchford/Design by Glenn Fretz
Printed in the United States of America

10 9 8 7 6 5 4 3 2

CONTENTS

12. The Ever-Changing New Order

List of Illustrations

Foreword

Conscience groups are essential in a democratic society. Minority cultures that question and at some points refuse to cooperate with excesses such as consumptive spending, pecuniary thinking, self praise, and waste of human resources are ultimately a great asset to the human community. Rare indeed are those communities who will regulate their technology in such a manner as to maximize their social patterns. People who place their faith in quality interpersonal relationships, and who deposit their trust in social rather than technological advances are ultimately a great asset to society.

The Amish communities represent a tradition of togetherness that is more genuinely cohesive than that of many rural communities in North America. They do not share in the present widespread alienation and identity confusion. They are a people without major identity problems, neither groping for answers to questions of ultimate meaning nor coercing society for a greater share of its economic goods. Their collective identity was formed during the Reformation period in the sixteenth century and still serves them well.

The dedication of the Amish to "keeping their own house in order" — the cultivation of proper inter-personal relations, bondedness, and community self-realization — has given rise to the view that they are conservers of the past. Through the practice of moderation they have indeed retained some of the finest qualities of community life. Throughout their history they have been willing to die for their principles and this ironically has made it possible for them to survive. They have no notions of building a utopian society on earth, for they profess to be strangers and sojourners. Their practices of "nonconformity to the world," their refusal to bear arms or swear oaths, or to accept government welfare, have sometimes been causes for misunderstandings. Gradually we are beginning to realize that the conflict over compulsory high school attendance is an unnecessary problem. Good government in a multi-cultural society has come to recognize that training children to become adults is the responsibility of parents and the community as well as the state, and that ultimate values are not wholly generated by departments of education.

This book encompasses not only the Old Order Amish, that wing of the movement typified by austere living, horse-and-buggy culture, but the whole of the Amish Mennonite settlements in Canada, including its more progressive counterparts. Unlike the Mennonites who came to Canada from the United States (in 1786) to flee from the militaristic spirit of the American revolution, the Amish came directly from Bavaria. It all began in 1822 when Christian Nafziger travelled to Amsterdam, New Orleans, Lancaster, and finally to Wilmot where the governor of Upper Canada under King George IV provided each immigrant Amish family with 200 acres of land. In doing so Canada opened its doors of hospitality to a quiet, peaceful people, deeply committed to the principles of mutual aid, community self-realization, moderation, and stewardship of the soil.

The author has a broad grasp of the historical movement and an intimate knowledge of the localized settlements of the Amish people in Ontario. **The Amish Of Canada** is the first major literary contribution on the Canadian Amish Mennonites. It will be a source of self knowledge for the Amish and Mennonite groups and for Canadians it will make possible a better understanding of the roots of cultural pluralism.

John A. Hostetler, **Professor of Anthropology and Sociology,**
Temple University, Philadelphia, Pa.

Preface

The following story of the Amish of Canada, now existing as an organized and separate group only in the province of Ontario represents the fulfillment of a promise made to the late Harold S. Bender, then dean of Goshen College Biblical Seminary in Indiana, U.S.A. While studying church history under Bender, one of the course requirements I had to meet was a 5000 word essay on some aspect of church history. When I expressed interest in writing about my own people but was fearful of not being able to meet the requirements for lack of data, Bender promised leniency, provided I continue the research and produce a more comprehensive history later.

A second round came with my completion of studies at the Evangelical Lutheran Seminary in Waterloo, Ontario. With strong encouragement from the late Dr. U. S. Leupold, dean of the seminary, further research was undertaken and the first chapter of the present work written. Family and vocational responsibilities prevented the completion of the project at that time. Since very little had been written on the subject previously, the historical task entailed much time-consuming research.

The final factor contributing to the completion of the work were the plans to commemorate the one hundred and fiftieth anniversary of the coming of the Amish pioneers to Canada from Europe. Fortunately, I found myself in circumstances which made it possible to contribute major blocks of time to the effort. However, as this goes to press I feel another year or two could have profitably been spent in further research. My feelings were pertinently expressed by a friend who recently commented, "When you write a book you never finish it, you simply abandon it."

A word needs to be said about sources. Although, as indicated, very little had been written, most helpful was a brief outline of the Amish congregations in Ontario by Jacob R. Bender and published in a history of the Mennonites in Ontario in 1935. Other sources included archival material at the Kitchener Public Library, Conrad Grebel College, Waterloo and provincial and federal archives at Toronto and Ottawa, respectively. For much of the material in Chapter X, I am indebted to Joseph Stoll and a paper he wrote on Recent Amish Immigration to Ontario, 1966.

Tribute must also be paid to the countless individuals whom the author interviewed and who cooperated by sharing family and church records, experiences, and personal knowledge of the past as handed down orally. The privilege of going through the personal records and conference material collected by Christian Brunk, long-time secretary of the Ontario Amish Mennonite Conference, was most helpful and greatly appreciated.

Other people who contributed much to the finished product were my brother, Alvin Gingerich, whose sharing of ideas and enthusiasm gave constant encouragement; and Norman and Eleanor High, who read the first draft of the script, made grammatical corrections and offered alternate readings. I am especially indebted to Dr. Frank H. Epp, who not only assumed responsibility for publication of the present volume, but also made many helpful suggestions relative to content, structure, and final format.

In addition Dave Kroeker, managing editor of the Mennonite Reporter, also did considerable work on the manuscript. Special thanks goes to Sylvia Gascho who did practically all the typing beginning with the first draft of the manuscript.

A serious attempt has been made to present the facts relating to the Amish of Canada. Should the reader discover errors, omissions, or other discrepancies I would appreciate hearing from you in the interests of a more authentic record for the future. If the present work does nothing more than bring out additional information it will have accomplished at least part of its purpose.

I am fully aware, however, that I have done much more than record the facts. Just as important as recording the facts — and perhaps much more important — is the task of interpreting. Why did things take place? What were the dynamics behind the sequence of events? These things are more difficult to ascertain than the facts themselves, and errors in judgment are easily made. I assume full responsibility for the interpretations as well as for the compilation of information. My views are naturally colored by my biases, despite an attempt to be fair and objective. They are submitted as a serious attempt to make the history of the Amish meaningful and instructive.

Hopefully, the following brief account will give the reader a clearer understanding of the Amish, the niche they occupy in the development of Canada, and their continuing contribution to Canadian Society. May the faith, courage, and virtues displayed by the pioneering forefathers provide new stimulus for all to emulate. The present frontier calling for pioneers probably relates more to the spirit than to geography. Both, this story of the Amish and the state-of-affairs in the world today, indicate a great need for exploration and development in the area of human relations. May the lessons learned from the past enable us to build a better future.

Orland Gingerich,
Baden, Ontario, Canada,
October 1, 1972.

The Beginnings In Europe

1

The Reformation

The story of the Amish people of Canada has its beginnings in Europe nearly three centuries ago. As an outgrowth of the Anabaptist and Mennonite movements, however, their history dates back 450 years to the Protestant Reformation. Their present faith and life cannot be understood without at least a brief flashback to that earlier time of beginnings.

When Luther hammered his 95 theses on the church door in Wittenberg he was little aware of the chain reaction he was setting off throughout Europe. For many years factors had been at work preparing the soil which made the Reformation possible. Luther's daring opposition to current religious practices and authority was to have repercussions far beyond his expectations. He had no intentions of starting a new church. He was simply agitating for the removal of some abuses. The ensuing discussions, however, resulted in an ever-widening doctrinal gap between Luther and his followers on one side and the existing church on the other. Biblicism and Catholic churchism could no longer be reconciled.

A few years later in Switzerland, Ulrich Zwingli, parish priest at the great Münster church in Zurich, was the instigator of another reform movement even more radical than Luther's in Germany. Whereas Luther retained most of the liturgy and practices of the Catholic church not expressly contrary to scripture, Zwingli abolished all things not actually commanded or practised in the New Testament church. Another more radical view related to Zwingli's concept of the sacraments. While Luther maintained that baptism and the Lord's supper actually conveyed grace to the recipient, Zwingli held that they were merely symbolic practices enjoined by Christ as commemorative signs.

Closely associated with Zwingli in Zurich was a young university graduate by the name of Conrad Grebel. Grebel was a loyal supporter of Zwingli's reform movement until the fall of 1523, when, after a public debate on the mass, Zwingli was willing to leave to the city council the final decision as to whether or not to continue the observance. Grebel objected on the basis that the Word of God, and not the city council, should be the final authority in spiritual matters. The final break with Zwingli came early in 1525 over the issue of infant baptism. Grebel and a number of his associates maintained that the only scriptural baptism was that performed on adults upon their personal profession of faith in Christ. Grebel's view on this point is probably best summarized by a statement he made in a public debate before the Zurich city council:

> "From these words of scripture it is clearly seen what baptism is and to whom baptism should be applied, namely, to one who has been converted by the Word of God, has changed his heart and henceforth desires to walk in newness of life. . . From this I have clearly learned and know assuredly that baptism means nothing else than a dying of the old man, and a putting on of the new man, and that Christ commanded to baptize those who had been taught. . . I should like to hear anyone who can show to me by clear and plain scripture that John, Christ, or the Apostles baptized children or taught that they should be baptized."

In affirming his belief that children are saved without water baptism Grebel said:

> "We hold that all children who have not yet come to discernment of the knowledge of good and evil, and have not yet eaten of the tree of knowledge, that they are surely saved by the suffering of Christ, the new Adam, who has restored their vitiated life, because they would have been subject to death and condemnation only if Christ had not suffered. . ."

However, Zwingli and the city council decided to continue infant baptism. Shortly after this it was made a criminal offence not to baptize infants. Nevertheless, on January 21, 1525, in a meeting at the home of Felix Manz, Grebel performed the first adult baptismal service of the Reformation. Thus began the Anabaptist movement. The term Anabaptist, meaning to baptize again, was a derisive one, and was applied to all who permitted themselves to be baptized as adults. It must be remembered that there were no unbaptized people in Europe at this time, since every infant was baptized in the Catholic church. Grebel and his associates became known as the Swiss brethren.

Conrad Grebel died of the plague in the summer of 1526. His associate, Felix Manz became the first Anabaptist martyr when he was drowned in Zurich in 1527. However, conditions for the Anabaptist protest were ripe. The movement soon spread all over Europe. In Holland in the town of Witmarsum a parish priest by the name of Menno Simons, after years of spiritual struggles, decided in 1536 to cast his lot with the Anabaptists. Menno became an underground evangelist, later an elder and outstanding leader among the persecuted and scattered believers. While Menno did considerable writing, his greatest contribution probably lay in his organizing ability. He is credited with drawing together the saner elements of the Anabaptist movement. After him its adherents became known as Mennonites.

For years the Anabaptists were persecuted mercilessly because of their radical ideas (for those times) of baptism upon a confession of faith (meaning a rejection of infant baptism), complete separation of church and state, the free or believers' church concept, and freedom of conscience in matters of religious belief. The persecution was also partly due to extremists who brought the whole movement into disrepute. Persecutions failed, however, to subdue the evangelistic fervor of the movement, and after years of harassment and perpetual flight the Mennonites settled down to organized congregational life. Largely through Menno's efforts a common basis of doctrine and practice was established, although dissension arose over matters of church discipline as early as the closing years of Menno's life.

With the Anabaptist emphasis on practical Christian living went a rather strict discipline. While the believers agreed with the Reformation emphasis on salvation by grace alone through faith, they maintained that if faith were genuine it would issue in good works. In other words, grace was manifest also in holy living and not only in forgiveness and justification. Any members, therefore, who slipped from the standards of New Testament scripture, as interpreted by the brotherhood, were first admonished according to Jesus' teaching (Matthew 18:15-20). If this admonition failed, they were excommunicated, and if still unrepentant, placed under the ban — a strict form of social ostracism aimed at bringing the transgressor back to the fold. Menno Simons held to a fairly strict interpretation of the ban, which he is said to have regretted in his later years.

Origin of the Amish

The application of the ban became the focal point of a controversy which gave rise to the Amish Mennonites. Jacob Amman, a young Swiss Mennonite bishop, originally from Erlenbach, Canton of Bern, found fault with an older bishop by the name of John Reist, for not excommunicating and placing under the ban a member of the church who had confessed to telling an untruth.

Unfortunately, very little is known of Jacob Amman's earlier life. The earliest record of his name ever discovered was in a state document recording all Anabaptists in the region of Saint-Marie-aux-Mines in Alsace and dated February 27, 1696. Since no record of his birth has been found it is assumed that his parents must have been Anabaptists because births were recorded by the church at baptism and not by the state. Interestingly, state church records indicate that a daughter of Jacob Amman, an Anabaptist minister, was baptized in the state church as an adult in 1730. The same document states that Amman was a native of Erlenbach, but that he had died before this time outside of Bern.

From letters extant written by Amman and a number of other ministers during the ensuing controversy, it is evident that Jacob Amman had lived in Alsace and the Palatinate previous to the debate on the ban. That he was influenced by the teaching and practices of the Mennonites in this area can be safely concluded from his attempts, before the debate on the ban, to introduce in the Swiss churches two practices common in Alsace but not in Switzerland. These practices were the observance of communion twice yearly, instead of only once, and the practice of foot-washing as an ordinance in connection with the communion service.

John Reist had apparently experienced some difficulty in his own congregation over these innovations spearheaded by Amman. Consequently, Reist paid scant attention to Amman and counselled others, "not to consider seriously the teaching and ordinances of youths." When Reist failed to appear for a second meeting called by Amman to discuss the issue, Amman is reported to have pulled a paper out of his pocket and read a list of six charges against the older bishop and pronounced him and all others who sided with him excommunicated. Thus began the Amish division. The foregoing evidence indicates that part of the problem was a personality clash between Amman and Reist, and that both share some of the blame for the resulting division. However, as is usually the case, doctrinal and practical matters became the actual issues over which the church split.

Amman later confessed to undue hastiness and rashness in his action, but unwilling to change his interpretation of scripture, the issue was never resolved. From the records of the debate it is evident that Amman's insistence on a more literal interpretation of scripture was another factor in the controversy. Let us examine the evidence more closely.

As indicated earlier, Amman began to conduct communion services twice yearly instead of once as heretofore in Switzerland. The two older bishops, John Reist and Benedict Schneider, opposed this innovation although it had apparently been decided to permit it. Thus Amman and Reist became the leaders of opposing factions which, in the ensuing discussion, soon included other matters. When Amman became aware that Reist did not practise the strict application of the ban as interpreted by the Dortrecht Confession of Faith, he accused Reist of not being true to scripture. The Dortrecht confession had been drawn up in 1632 at a Mennonite convention, but was never officially recognized by the Swiss Mennonites. The article of this confession referred to by Amman reads:

> "Concerning the withdrawing from or shunning the separated, we believe and confess, that if any one either through his wicked life or perverted doctrine, has so far fallen that he is separated from God, and, consequently, also separated and punished by the church, the same must, according to the doctrine of Christ and His Apostles, be shunned without distinction, by all the fellow members of the church, especially those to whom, in eating, drinking, and other similar intercourse, and no company be had with him, that they may not become contaminated by intercourse with him, nor made partaker of his sins; but that the sinner may be ashamed, pricked in his heart, and convicted in his conscience, unto his reformation (I Corinthians 5:9-11; II Thessalonians 3:14). Yet in shunning as well as in reproving, such moderation and Christian discretion be used, that it may conduce, not to destruction, but to the reformation of the sinner. For, if he is needy, hungry, thirsty, naked, or sick, or in any other distress, we are in duty bound, necessity requiring it, according to love and the doctrine of Christ and His Apostles, to render him aid and assistance; otherwise, shunning would in this case tend more to destruction than to reformation.
>
> Therefore we must not count them as enemies, but admonish them as brethren, that thereby they may be brought to a knowledge of and to repentance and sorrow for their sins, so that they may

become reconciled to God, and, consequently be received again into the church; and that love may continue with them according as is proper" (II Thessalonians 3:15).

Amman insisted that not eating and drinking referred to all social intercourse, whereas Reist and his followers held that scripture referred only to the communion service in this case. Taking three ministers with him, Amman toured other Swiss churches to determine what the ministers believed about the ban. Discovering that only a few agreed with him, he decided to call a meeting of all Swiss ministers to discuss the issue. Most came, but John Reist was conspicuously absent. Another meeting was called for two weeks hence with Amman through intermediaries, especially requesting Reist's presence. Reist ignored the meeting and in the meantime wrote a letter to the churches rejecting Amman's view and suggesting that his readers not pay too much attention to him. Aware of this action and no doubt deeply hurt by Reist's refusal to discuss the issue, Amman in a second meeting read off six charges against Reist and pronounced him excommunicated. Some of his colleagues tried to dissuade Amman from his rash action, but according to the Reist party Amman would not listen and left the meeting with his followers. Thus the decision was formalized. This meeting took place in the summer of 1693.

The letter from which Amman read his six charges against Reist has apparently not been preserved, and so we have no way of knowing what the actual charges were. However, from other letters extant, other issues which also figured in the controversy included attendance at state church services, attitude toward those who were apparently sincere in their Christian beliefs but remained in the state church, and stricter regulations in matters pertaining to dress.

Returning to the sequence of events following the divisive meeting recounted above, we note that the followers of Amman began to meet separately, and Amman himself apparently moved to Alsace where he received more support for his views than in his native Switzerland. Most of the Mennonites in Alsace had originally come from Switzerland, having fled from that country earlier to escape severe persecution. The Swiss Mennonites, on the other hand, wrote a letter to the churches in the Palatinate requesting help in resolving the conflict. On October 16, 1693 a number of Palatinate ministers wrote to the Amish pleading with them to seek reconciliation. A few ministers from Alsace had apparently also written to the Palatinate for counsel relative to the division. However, later in the same year Amman sent a warning letter (**War-**

nungsschrift) to all churches requesting that they either report to him their acceptance of his views or prove him wrong from the scriptures. Amman set a deadline for a reply by March 7, 1694. All persons who had not reported by this time were to be excommunicated.

The ministers from the Palatinate arranged for a meeting in Alsace early in March of 1694 to attempt a reconcilation. Ministers from the three areas, Switzerland, the Palatinate, and Alsace were present. However, no agreement was reached and the Amish left the meeting. On the following day the Swiss and Palatinate ministers drafted a joint statement explaining why they could not agree with Amman and that "for this reason we cannot, and do not desire to retain him (Amman) or those affiliated with him as brethren and sisters." Thus an excommunication was followed by a counter-excommunication finalizing the division. As a result, most of the Alsatian churches and a few from the Palatinate and Switzerland followed Amman while the majority in these latter countries repudiated his views.

Attempts at reconciliation were made periodically until 1711 but no lasting results were achieved. As indicated earlier, at one point Amman and his followers confessed to overly rash action in excommunicating others without the consent of the brotherhood. They asked to be received into the church again. They even went so far as to excommunicate themselves and place themselves under the ban. However, they continued to insist on the strict observance of the ban and on practising footwashing as an ordinance. Negotiations broke down and no reconciliation was achieved.

The Amish in Europe

Since the division occasioned by the Amman-Reist controversy, the followers of Jacob Amman were officially known as Amish Mennonites. Frequently they were referred to simply as Amish. As the movement crystalized the Amish developed certain distinctive characteristics. Their more conservative stance on clothing soon made them easily recognizable from their Mennonite counterparts. The required wearing of beards, without a moustache, as well as hooks and eyes rather than buttons to fasten their clothing were the most obvious distinguishing features.

Their distinctivenss in matters relating to church life was most evident in their strict observance of the Meidung, or ban, referred to earlier. Possibly as a reaction against

Amman's vain attempt to force his views on the entire church, the Amish developed a very congregation-centered type of church government. Also a seeming contradiction to Amman's original attitude, is their very strong emphasis on humility. More in line with his emphasis is the importance and authority of the bishop in Amish church polity. Otherwise they shared the typical Anabaptist-Mennonite views and teachings of the time.

Being of Swiss-German descent the Amish exhibited traits typical of their social and cultural background. Generally speaking, they were of peasant stock and for the most part farmers, although there were some artisans and tradesmen. Records indicate that prior to their coming to Canada there were bakers, millers, wagon-makers, and even physicians among them. In Europe they had acquired an excellent reputation as farmers. Noblemen often welcomed them to their estates, although not always with the best of motives. They were known to be hard-working, thrifty, and honest. Their deep religious convictions and high moral standards enhanced many of their natural and cultural endowments.

Another factor common to the Amish in Europe were their frequent migrations. For the most part these migrations were the result of circumstances, religious persecution, and edicts banishing them from certain areas. Sometimes envious neighbours resented their special privileges, such as exemption from military service, or were jealous of the prosperity the Amish enjoyed when permitted to exercise their abilities. In the following paragraphs an attempt is made to trace briefly these migrations in Europe.

The country of Alsace probably contained the largest population of Amish in the eighteenth century. In 1712 King Louis XV ordered the Amish expelled from Alsace. Some migrated to the neighbouring Palatinate and Baden, others went to Montbéliard, while still others located in Lorraine. Still later small Amish congregations were established in France itself. During the time of the first French Republic the Amish fared well under French rule.

In Germany the Amish settled in the Hesse-Cassel region, near Woldech and Morburg, in addition to the Palatinate. Another migration from the Palatinate, Alsace, and Lorraine took the Amish to the regions of Ingoldstadt, Regensburg, and Munich in Bavaria.

Two congregations were established by the Amish in Holland about 1750. These were located at Groningen and Kampen. They continued a separate existence untill about 1850 when they were absorbed into the surrounding Mennonite congregations.

In 1785 a number of Amish families settled in Galicia at the invitation of the Austrian emperor, Joseph II. Later in 1803 these families and others established a settlement in Volhynia, a province of Western Russia where several congregations were subsequently established. However, most of these migrated to the United States in 1875. Apparently poor soil, high taxes and other related matters were responsible for the move.

In Switzerland, Amman's native country, the Amish were located in two main areas, the Emmental and Jura regions. The Amish population of that country was never very large and was further reduced by emigration to other countries in Europe as well as to North America in the late 18th and early 19th centuries. The congregations that did remain gradually lost their identity and by the end of the 19th century were absorbed into the Swiss Mennonite Conference.

Early in the present century the last Amish congregations in Europe were absorbed back into the Mennonite church. Today no distinctive Amish congregations remain anywhere in Europe. Those who did not migrate to America merged with the Mennonites. North America is the only place the Amish have maintained their separate identity. In the past decade several settlements of Amish have also been established in Central and South America. These, however, have come from North America, principally from the United States.

Reasons for Migrations

Probably the most frequent reason for the Amish migrations in Europe was religious persecution. Their Anabaptist forefathers had been mercilessly persecuted in the 16th century. While the severity of this persecution had abated somewhat in the 17th century, the Anabaptists were still despised and maligned for their religious beliefs well into the 18th century.

By 1700, when the Amish had become a distinct group, it was not always easy to separate the religious from the economic reasons for persecution. As indicated earlier, the Amish had proved themselves adept at transforming war damaged countryside into productive farm lands. More than one nobleman or petty ruler welcomed them to his land for this main reason, only to expel them later when it was to his economic advantage. Sometimes a change in political leadership resulted in a new wave of persecution. In most of these forced migrations the Amish had to abandon everything except what they could physically carry.

Some of the moves were obviously instigated by the Amish themselves in an attempt to better themselves economically. At other times the promise of greater religious freedom beckoned them to distant places. The latter two factors appear to have played a large part in their coming to this continent. Even though material gain was not the primary motivating objective, they were concerned about providing the necessities of life for themselves and their families. In light of the economic hardships and unsettled type of existence they experienced in Europe it is small wonder that the thought of a virgin country where they could own their own land and where there was at least the prospect of economic improvement, should provide an incentive strong enough for them to brave the rigours of migration and pioneering.

The most immediate reason for the Amish migration to Canada beginning in 1822 was the militarism and forced conscription of the Napoleonic era. One of the distinctive Anabaptist-Mennonite-Amish beliefs has always been that of love and non-resistance. This belief has found positive expression in mutual sharing of material things with any brother in need — indeed, not only with fellow church members, but with anyone in need regardless of race, colour or creed.

On the other hand, it has led to the rejection of the use of force. Warfare in all its forms has always been looked upon as contrary to the principles of the New Testament. Oral tradition in the Amish community in Ontario makes military conscription the primary reason for emigration to Canada. This is a very plausible reason, not only in light of their theological convictions, but also because of the historical-political situation which confronted the Amish in Europe following 1800.

Napoleon is credited with conscripting over two million men into his army between 1800 and 1813. Documents in European archives provide evidence that the Amish frequently petitioned the authorities for exemption from military duties. At times such exemption was granted, at other times it was denied. Usually it included the payment of special taxes or fines in lieu of actual service. However, it was not only military service which prompted emigration. Frequent wars between Germany and France in which the Palatinate and Alsace-Lorraine became the battle ground no doubt encouraged the Amish to look elsewhere for a place to settle.

The Amish aversion to the militarism of the Napoleonic

era was not the only reason for their emigration to Canada. The tremendous changes sweeping over Europe in the late 18th and early 19th centuries as a result of the French Revolution also played a part in loosening the Amish from their homeland. This factor had special significance in light of the traditional Amish aversion to change. The political upheavals and the anti-religious mood then current in Europe threw into bold relief the prospect of living in virgin territory, separated from the "world" and its evil influences.

Furthermore, the Amish were at least somewhat accustomed to pulling up stakes and moving and so held lightly any earthly holdings or possessions. The twin prizes of freedom and peace were to them priceless possessions for which no cost was too high. Above all they and their children wanted to live in peace and have the freedom to live and worship according to the dictates of their conscience. This conscience was shaped by their interpretation of the Christian scriptures.

The earliest migration of Amish to North America occurred early in the 18th century. By 1740 a sizeable settlement existed in Lancaster County, Pennsylvania. Small off-shoots of this settlement were established further west in the same state. By 1810 the Amish had settled as far west as Fairfield and Holmes Counties in Ohio. Conditions in Europe as well as the Revolutionary War in America prevented any further migrations until after 1812. The Ontario settlement was only one of a number of North American settlements fed by the post-revolutionary stream of Amish immigrants. The original settlement in Ontario was the only one in Canada until the turn of the century.

Pioneer Settlement In Ontario

2

The Christian Nafziger Story

Following the reign of Napoleon and during the time when the Amish and thousands of other Europeans were hoping for new opportunities, an area across the sea known as Upper Canada was opening for settlement. Thousands of new colonists, known as loyalists, had entered the area during and immediately after the American Revolution. Among them were about 2,000 Mennonites, most of them picking Waterloo and Woolwich Townships of Waterloo County as their new home.

To the west lay additional rich farmlands waiting to be cleared of the dense forest then covering most of south-western Ontario. The region was variously known as Canada West, Gore District, and after 1840 as Wellington District. In the early 1820s the land immediately west of Waterloo Township was named Wilmot Township in honor of the Deputy Surveyor, Samuel Street Wilmot.

Back to Europe. The time was 1821. The place, a humble Amish home in Bavaria, Germany. To Christian Nafziger, a peasant farmer, the future looked bleak and hopeless. Under existing conditions Nafziger found it difficult to support his family with his meager earnings. For days perhaps months, Christian and his wife had been wrestling with the possibilities, and the risks, involved in looking for a new home across the seas, possibly in William Penn's colony where some Amish from Europe had settled almost a century earlier.

Finally the painful decision was made. Christian would leave his family and strike out to investigate the possibilities. But how and with what? Nafziger had no money for such a venture, but he had faith in God and confidence in his fellowmen to help him in time of need. He travelled to Amsterdam, no doubt visiting some Amish friends in Holland en route. These friends helped him secure passage on a boat bound for New Orleans where he arrived in January of 1822.

From New Orleans Nafziger travelled to Pennsylvania hoping to find a place to which he could bring his family and friends. But alas, by this time the price of land in the state was too high for a poor peasant farmer from Europe. However, his spiritual brethren had a suggestion which brought a new ray of hope. There was cheap land available in Canada, although one had to be wary of such offers as some Mennonites from Pennsylvania had discovered 20 years earlier.

Once again Nafziger was supplied with money and a horse as he set out to investigate this newest possibility. He arrived in the Waterloo County Mennonite settlement in August of 1822. Leaders with whom he conferred suggested the possibility of purchasing land immediately west of their own holdings. Aware that the proposed site for the new settlement was Crown land reserved for the King, the Mennonites directed Nafziger to the Governor of Upper Canada in York (now Toronto). Governor Maitland agreed to sell a block of land to all the German settlers Nafziger would bring. Each settler was promised 50 acres of free land provided he would clear a two-rod strip along the front of a 200 acre plot, build a cabin and pay a small surveyor's fee. The settler could purchase the additional 150 acres of his plot at a later date for $2.50 an acre.

Nafziger's faith in God and confidence in his brethren was more than substantiated. He began his homeward journey with assurance from his Mennonite friends in Waterloo County that they would do all they could to assist the new Amish immigrants get established on their chosen property. To play it safe, Nafziger stopped off in London to have his agreement with Governor Maitland ratified. King George IV, being himself of German descent, assured Nafziger of the reliability of the Governor's offer. A story concerning Nafziger's visit to King George, published in a local weekly newspaper at the time of Nafziger's death in 1836, indicates that the King pressed a few gold coins into Nafziger's hand as he bade him goodbye and wished him and his fellow countrymen success in their venture.

Travelling back, probably through Alsace-Lorraine and the Palatinate, to his home in Bavaria, Nafziger spread the good news of his "land find" in Canada. Although he was unable to return for several years, Amish from the above named countries began to arrive in Canada in 1824. In the meantime Nafziger had apparently sent word of his good fortune to Pennsylvania as well for colonists began arriving from that state even before many European Amish came.

The First Settlement

Following Nafziger's visit a number of steps were taken to prepare for the new German settlers. Possibly even before Nafziger's departure Mennonite settlers in Waterloo Township agreed to oversee the settlement of Wilmot. This committee included Abraham Erb, Jacob Erb, Samuel Eby, and Jacob C. Snider. Governor Maitland gave orders to have the German Block, as it was now called, surveyed. This was done in 1823. Two hundred acre plots were laid out along three roads running west of already existing Waterloo Township roads. These roads were Erb Street, Snyders Road (now 7 & 8 highway) and Bleams Road. The German settlers soon renamed the roads "Oberstrasse" (Upper Street), "Mittelstrasse" (Middle Street), and "Unterstrasse" (Lower Street).

A few Amish immigrants came from Pennsylvania. However, most of these had arrived in that state from Europe only a few years previously. When word of Nafziger's agreement with Canadian authorities reached Pennsylvania, a number of such families decided to migrate. Concerned for the spiritual welfare of the new colony, Bishop John Stoltzfus ordained several men, probably before they left Pennsylvania, to assume the spiritual oversight of the new settlement. Joseph Goldschmidt and John Brenneman were ministers and Jacob Kropf was the deacon. Kropf settled on Lot 13, Snyders Road North, Goldschmidt on Lot 14 next to Kropf, and Brenneman on Lot 13, Bleams Road South.

More will be said about the ministry later, but it must be remembered that Amish community was never complete without the ordained spiritual leaders. They were spokesmen for the faith and defenders of Amish orthodoxy. They were the anchormen of the community, at least as long as everybody agreed. If and when differences of opinions developed with or within the leadership, these differences could not easily be resolved without migration or some other division in the community.

The very first family to arrive from Pennsylvania was, as far as is known, the Michael Schwartzentruber family. They settled on Lot 9, Snyders Road South. Also coming about the same time were a number of other families from the same state who were not Amish but German Methodist, or Evangelical, as they were officially known by this time. Several of these families settled on the Bleams Road where some of their descendants still reside. Early family names in this group were Hammacher, Siebert, Wilfong, and Gabel.

From 1825 on, the Amish from Europe began arriving in a steady stream. Christian Nafziger finally came back bringing his family and some friends. He settled on Lot 6, Bleams Road North, the northeast lot at the intersection of Bleams Road and the Petersburg-New Dundee highway. Coming with Nafziger was a minister, Christian Steinman, who settled on Lot 18, Snyders Road North where the Wilmot congregation later built its first meeting house. Also in the same group was Peter Nafziger, a bishop. He served as the first resident bishop until 1831 when he emigrated to Ohio.

A number of other families migrated to Ohio in that year, accompanied by Joseph Goldschmidt and Christian Fahrni. Fahrni had been ordained in 1829, as had another man, John Oesch. The latter had settled on Lot 14, Snyders Road North on what is now known as the Livingston farm. After Bishop Peter Nafziger left for Ohio, Oesch was ordained to take his place. Some of the other families who moved to Ohio in 1831 later settled in Illinois.

In 1829 the deputy surveyor Samuel Wilmot was asked to inspect the new settlement in Wilmot Township and report to Mr. Robinson, the commissioner of crown lands. Apparently the said crown land had been given over to King's College in York (Toronto), an Anglican school and forerunner of the University of Toronto. In Wilmot's report to Robinson he indicated that the settlers complained about the price of land, as set by the Governors of the College, at 20 shillings instead of the 12 shillings, six pence promised by Governor Maitland. Wilmot recommended that the original price be adhered to. Another complaint registered was that many of the settlers had not received their deeds and some not even a location ticket. Wilmot also scored some "monied men" from Waterloo who had claimed lots and were holding them for speculation, "much to the injury of the poor persons who wished to become actual settlers in Wilmot, an evil the inhabitants are desirous to have checked, as such proceedings retard the settlement of the Township."

As to the settlers themselves, Wilmot described them as "very industrious, and peaceable Dutch settlers, who emigrated from Germany and Pennsylvania a few years ago." He further stated that about 50 plots were taken up at that time. Not nearly all the roads were cleared of trees as was stipulated in the contract, but he excused the settlers on the basis that it was essential for them to clear land for crops first to produce the necessary food supply.

In addition to Wilmot's written report to the commissioner of crown lands were the "returns" or tables, — now located in the Ottawa archives — indicating the name of each settler in 1829 and the particular lot on which each lived. Amish family names appearing in these tables included the following: Schwartzentruber, Goldschmidt, Brenneman, Boshart, Gingerich, Hondrich, Lichty, Kropf, Roth, Kipfer, Ruby, Mayer, Fahrni, Miller, Steinman, Sommer, Nafziger, Schultz, Ropp, Erb, Oesch, Gardner, Wismer, Litwiller, Helmuth and Unsicker.

Some of these family names no longer appear among the Amish of Ontario. Others were added as new settlers arrived after 1829. Besides the Evangelical Germans from Pennsylvania, Lutheran and Catholic settlers from Alsace-Lorraine and South Germany also made their homes in Wilmot Township. As the first white settlers in the area and the first Germans coming directly from Europe, the Amish triggered this new wave of German immigrants to Canada. Most of these people were also of peasant background. They too found life in Europe difficult due to their social status and the frequent changes of the "state religion" from Protestant to Catholic and vice versa. News of the opportunities in Canada was no doubt shared by the Amish with their neighbors in Europe.

Pioneer Life

Most of the early Amish settlers who came to Canada were young people, although there were also some middle aged folks among them. The reasons for this are fairly obvious. The rigors of travel in those days, plus the need to chop their homes and farms out of the virgin forest were obstacles only the young, strong, and brave would venture to overcome. The trip across the Atlantic was made by sailboat. Depending on the winds, the crossing usually took from six weeks to several months. Stories have been handed down of the hardships endured en route. They included days of severe storms until almost everybody on board despaired of life. Premature births, seasickness, days of aimless drifting or struggling against adverse elements tried the courage and faith of the most dauntless.

After arriving in America and disembarking usually at Baltimore, Philadelphia, or New York, a long hard journey overland still lay ahead. Some of the immigrants walked most of these hundreds of miles. Some were able to purchase a horse, or team and wagon, from some of their brethren in Pennsylvania, which made the trip somewhat easier. But even at best, the roads were poor with very few bridges and very few inns or other accommodation along the way.

The earliest settlers in Wilmot usually left their wives and families with Mennonite settlers in Waterloo until they had erected a cabin on their plots in Wilmot. The men would frequently stay in the woods for days at a time, making tree-houses to sleep in at night. Typical were the Gingerich and Hondrich families. Married in 1824 in Europe the two brothers-in-law came to Canada the following year. Locating on two adjoining plots on Bleams Road North, just south of the present town of Baden, the two men set to work immediately building log cabins and clearing land.

Each family built their cabin on an elevation with a spring creek flowing between them, a good source of fresh water. Next the men chopped down the trees between the two cabins which were situated about half a mile apart. This provided land for planting crops and permitted a clear view from one cabin to the other, making the wilderness a little less foreboding. It must be remembered that at this time there were no roads, and the nearest town, if it can be called that, was Ebytown, later Berlin, then Kitchener. Except for a few Indian trails the area was a trackless forest.

Apparently there were few native Canadians in Wilmot or the neighboring townships in which the Amish settled. There was an encampment of Indians on the shore of what later came to be called Hofstetler's Lake just southeast of the Baden hills. The writer recalls hearing a great uncle tell the story of how his parents told of Indians coming to the Schwartzentruber cabin to trade venison for bread and apple butter. The Indians would frequently take young Michael Schwartzentruber along on their hunting trips and teach him to shoot game with bow and arrow. Some of the Amish who moved to Perth and Oxford Counties a little later also had some contacts with natives in that area. These contacts seem, however, to have been infrequent, possibly because of the rather small number of Indians in this part of the country. Relations with the natives seem to have been most cordial.

Needless to say the life of the early settlers in Ontario was strenuous and the comforts few. The first cabins were invariably one-room homes with the crudest of homemade furnishings. Heating in the winter was by open fireplace. This is also where the cooking and baking was done. Tales of men carrying a bag of wheat ten to 20 miles to have it ground into flour are not uncommon.

The earliest tillage tools were made of wood, and most of the tilling was done by hand. A little later oxen and horses provided power for working the soil. Harvesting crops in those early years also entailed hard hand labor. Even after the grain and hay fields became fairly large they were still cut with scythe and cradle. The grain was bound into sheaves by hand, using a few stalks of grain twisted together as a band. Threshing and winnowing was also done by hand.

However, work was usually made lighter because there were many hands to do it. Neighbors usually got together to do the major tasks. Most Amish families were large — a real asset in pioneer days. In addition new settlers were always arriving, many of whom were only too glad to obtain employment with those already established.

Amish women often assisted with outside work. This was particularly true of the younger women. The vegetable garden was generally cared for by the feminine members of the home. There was always the cooking, not only for the family but also for hired help and working crews at "bees". In addition to making and mending clothes there was butter and cheese to make and food to preserve for the long winter ahead. Sometimes a woman's work called not only for strength but also for courage. Hearing a noise in the pig pen one day, great-grandmother Gingerich went to investigate and found a bear after the year's supply of pork. Arming herself with a hickory stick she hustled the bear off into the woods and thus saved the winter's supply of meat.

Pioneer life was not all work and no play. Despite their rather somber appearance the Amish have a keen sense of humor and generally a very wholesome outlook on life. Some of their wisdom sayings illustrate this point very well, sayings like: "schpaas en ehrra kan ahm niemond vorwehra." Although untranslatable in English, the saying means essentially that harmless fun or jokes are not wrong. Working bees were usually spiked with jokes, tricks, and harmless banter. Hunting and fishing provided not only food for the larder but also recreation.

Another aspect of Amish life is the emphasis on socializing so characteristic of their culture as well as their faith. The bi-weekly worship services were great occasions of fellowship. For the first 60 years these services were held in the homes and were always followed by a fellowship meal together at the home where the service was held. The Sunday between services was given to visiting friends or relatives or sick members. In the not-so-busy seasons of the year, people took time off to visit on week-days. Besides religious holidays weddings and funerals were always big social events, which, in the early years included the entire community.

Most of the Amish came to this country relatively poor. While part of the reason for coming was to better themselves economically, their main purpose was certainly not to become rich. That they worked hard to supply their own needs hardly needs repeating. However, they were really more interested in the quality of life rather than a quantity of things. That many of them did become moderately prosperous must be credited to their thrift. From about 1850 on, the log cabins were replaced with larger homes of frame construction, field stone, and brick, many of which still stand as a monument to the forefathers' hard work, thrift, and vision for the future.

Additional Settlements

South Easthope and East Zorra

As more settlers arrived from Europe the Amish community spread westward. Late in the twenties and early in the thirties the Amish began to purchase land beyond the Nith river (then known as Smith's Creek) in what is now South Easthope and East Zorra Townships, the former in Perth County and the latter in Oxford County. No doubt the early road system was largely responsible for this westward move. In addition to the three east-west roads of Wilmot Township mentioned earlier, the Huron Road running from Dundas to Goderich was opened in 1828. This road runs one block south of Bleams Road turning north at the westerly limits of the township to Snyders Road and then proceeds west through Stratford to Goderich. In time it became a main stage coach route. Furthermore, the fertile soil of the two townships was also a vital factor in drawing the Amish westward. Besides settling along the Huron Road the Amish located even more along the townline between Oxford and Perth towards the town of Tavistock.

The East Zorra congregation was organized in 1837. The first ordained men in this congregation came from Europe. They were Nichlaus Roth, a deacon from Alsace, and Peter Zehr, who was ordained in Lorraine. Zehr was also a licensed doctor and surgeon and was popularly known as Doctor Zehr. Some of the older people have indicated that his need to serve the sick on Sundays sometimes caused disruption in the services and contentions among the members. From lack of evidence to the contrary it is assumed that oversight of the congregation by a bishop was supplied by the Wilmot congregation until the decade following 1850.

Some of the distinctive family names appearing quite early in this congregation were: Ruby, Schlatter, Schlegel, Jausie, Schrag, Wutherich, Otto, Eicher, Eiman, Ingold, Zimmerman, Baechler, and Sommer. In addition to these were many others that appear in Wilmot as well. On the other hand, the following family names have disappeared from the current membership of the East Zorra church: Wutherich, Otto, Schlatter, Eicher, Eiman, Ingold, Zimmerman, and Jausie. A few of these still appear in the community but most of them have disappeared completely. A number of these families moved to the United States later in the 19th century.

The first ministers to be ordained in the East Zorra congregation were Daniel Schrag and Joseph Wutherich in 1849. In 1852 Joseph Ruby also received ordination. In the same year, Joseph Baechler, a minister ordained in France, moved into the community. Ordained with Ruby in 1852 was John Wagler as deacon. The following year Joseph Ruby was ordained as the first resident bishop of the church. He lived till 1897.

It is difficult to assess the membership of this congregation during this time. Figures from an Oxford County census conducted in 1852 indicate there were 159 Mennonites in the county. This figure does not include the Amish who resided in South Easthope Township, Perth County, and who were also members of East Zorra. From these figures one could safely conclude that the actual Amish population of the congregation reached several hundred at this time, with the actual adult membership considerably less. The Wilmot congregation probably remained the largest during this period of time.

Hay and Stanley Townships

The third area in which the Amish settled was in Huron County, Ontario. In 1848 Bishop John Oesch from Wilmot moved to Hay Township. Previous to this and possibly soon after the Huron Road was opened in 1828, some Mennonite families had arrived in this area and settled on the Goshen Line Road south of the present town of Zurich. The Amish moved north and west of the same town, as far north as Stanley Township. By the 1870s the following names appeared in the Amish congregation: Oesch, Brenneman, Schwartzentruber, Gingerich, Gascho, Jutzi, Baechler, Erb, Eicher, Mayer, Ingold, Bender, Kropf, Kuepfer, Kennel and Gerber. Wutherichs and Eglis, who had come from East Zorra, had by this time moved to Illinois. For some reason the Mennonite congregation on the Goshen Line Road did not prosper and the church house which they had built there was closed. A few of these families continued with the Amish congregation. The names Schantz and Steckley appear in an old church record dating back to 1875. Steckley could have been an Amish name, but Schantz is definitely not.

The Amish settled mostly on the Bronson Line, one road west of the Goshen Line Road. Just east of the Goshen Line is the Babylon Line Road. An account in a Huron County atlas explains how these roads were named. The Bronson Road was named after an early settler. Goshen is a biblical name, referring to that area in Egypt in which the children of Israel lived during their stay in that country. Mostly Protestants settled on this road, refusing to allow Catholics to locate there. The Catholics consequently took up land on the road immediately to the east which the Protestants then dubbed the "Babylon" road. Babylon is of course also a biblical word referring to one of Israel's enemies, and in the Book of Revelation symbolizes the height of evil upon which God would pass judgment. It was common practice during the protestant Reformation to accuse the Catholic church of being "Babylon" and to name the pope the antichrist.

There were, of course, counter-accusations by the Catholics. However, in Huron County the Protestant interpretation seemed to stick despite the fairly large Catholic settlement in the area. The author is happy to report, however, that relations have improved among the denominations. In the last several years churches of the district, including the Catholics, have cooperated in a series of joint worship services.

Besides Bishop Oesch, other ministers who served in this congregation in the early years include Joseph Wutherich and John Egli who moved to Illinois about 1860. Daniel Oesch and John D. Bender served for a time, but for reasons not yet discovered both were censured by the church and consequently left the congregation. Christian Schantz and Jacob Gingerich served as deacons in the early years of the church.

There seem to have been some problems in the congregation from the beginning. The church had no resident bishop following the death of Oesch in 1850. This is most unusual for an Amish congregation. Apparently it frequently happened that a number of members who lived in the north end of the community met separately for worship and prayer. This is frowned on in Amish tradition where equality and brotherhood are stressed. The group was accused of trying to be more pious than the rest. From the record it appears that most of the ministers either moved away or were censured, as indicated above. Still later there were more problems which we will look at in later chapters. The congregation was never very large but could have reached 100 or more persons by 1875.

Wellesley Township

This congregation was organized in 1859, about ten years after the one in Hay Township. Although close to Wilmot Township no congregation was organized here earlier, because Wellesley was a clergy reserve area. In a British Act of Parliament of 1793 one-seventh of the land in Canada had been set aside for the support of the clergy and another seventh for the crown. The clergy reserves, as they were called, quite early became a rather prickly problem for the government. When the reserves were finally dispensed with in 1854, settlement of the township began in earnest. The southeast section was soon bought up by the Amish and German settlers.

The first known Amish-man in the township was Christian Boshart. Other Amish names appearing in the county register as having purchased property in this period are: Roth, Leis, Schmidt, Gerber, Honderich, Kuepfer, Kennel, Miller, Jantzi, Schwartzentruber, Zehr, Streicher, Lichti, Jausie, and Reschley.

The Amish settlement spread westward toward the town of Wellesley, or Smithville (Schmidtsville), so called in honor of an early squatter in the township. The Amish continued to settle along the Third Line, as well as along the two roads north and south along the Fifth Line and to the town line between Wellesley and North Easthope in Perth County. In 1867 the congregation built a funeral chapel on the Third Line on the site of the congregation's cemetery. This chapel was of frame construction in contrast to a log structure built by the Wilmot and East Zorra congregations ten years earlier, and had a wood floor whereas the first building had a dirt floor. Additional family names appearing in this congregation were: Erb, Gascho, Schultz, Wagler, Lebold, Kuepfer, and Schlegel. Some of these names have disappeared and others have been added in more recent times.

Ministers serving the congregation when it was organized in 1859 included John Jantzi, who had settled in Lewis County, N.Y., after arriving from Lorraine. He had been ordained in that state in 1834. He apparently moved to Canada the following year and was ordained bishop in 1859 to serve the newly organized congregation in Wellesley. John Jausie and Joseph Lichti were apparently ordained before the congregation was organized but served here from the beginning. John Gerber was ordained deacon in 1859. Although it is almost impossible to give an accurate estimation of the size of the congregation by 1870, it would have been over 100 since a new congregation was organized further northwest a few years later.

Mornington, Ellice, and Elma

Naturally, Mornington Township was the first of the three townships to be settled since it bordered immediately to the west of Wellesley Township. A Perth County history suggests that one of the first settlers was Christian Kuepfer, who came into the area in 1860. Joseph Steckley is said to have settled in Elma in 1865. One of the most aggressive of the early pioneers in the area was Menno Schultz. Schultz built a saw mill, bought acres of crown land, cleared it and sold it again to new settlers. He was apparently something of a financial wizard, borrowing money extensively to finance his operations, usually having more than 20 men working for him. He worked out a formula for calculating the amount of interest he owed the bank so accurately that the banker in Stratford asked for his method. Like most of the more progressive Amishmen he did get into trouble with his brethren but stayed in the church nonetheless.

In addition to the family names suggested above, the following were also listed in the congregation in its early years: Nafziger, Ropp, Gerber, Schmidt, Albrecht, Roth, Schwartzentruber, Kropf, Brunk and Spenler. Since its organization took place only in 1874 the membership by 1875 could not have been very large. It must be remembered, however, that the Amish were living in the area ten years previously and were members of the Wellesley congregation before the congregation here was organized. It is more than likely that there were several dozen families who became charter members of the church in this community.

The early leadership of the Mornington congregation was composed of three ordained men. Joseph Gerber, who had been ordained minister in 1865 became the first bishop of the congregation when he was ordained to that office in 1875. Joseph U. Ropp, ordained in 1873, was the first minister, while John Kuepfer was ordained deacon later the same year.

Table I
Summary of Original Amish Settlement-Congregations

Name*	Date	Origin	Bishops
Wilmot Waterloo County	1824	Pennsylvania Europe	Peter Nafziger (1825-1831) John Oesch (1831-1848)
East Zorra Oxford County also Perth	1837	Europe Wilmot	 Joseph Ruby (1853-1897)
Hay Huron County	1848	Wilmot East Zorra	John Oesch (1818-1850)
Wellesley Waterloo County	1859	Europe Wilmot	John Jantzi (1859-1881)
Mornington Perth County	1874	Wilmot Europe East Zorra	Joseph Gerber (1875-1893)

*Name indicates location, since congregational settlements were known by the townships.

With the establishment of a congregation in Mornington Township the five original Amish communities in Ontario were completed. Each congregation came to be known by the township in which it was located — the Wilmot, East Zorra, Hay, Wellesley and Mornington congregations (see Table 1). Although a few immigrants continued to arrive after 1875, by far the greatest number had arrived prior to that date. There continued to be some shifting between the communities, particularly from the older to the newer ones, until after the turn of the century.

Portraits of Pioneers

There were a number of rather colorful personalities among the Amish pioneers in Canada. The following is only a partial glimpse, the stories of others having been lost in antiquity. Others have already been referred to in this chapter, people such as Dr. Zehr of the East Zorra congregation and Menno Schultz of Poole, who made unique contributions to the communities in which they lived.

Paul Bunyan-type tales have been passed on about Nick Schlegel, who was noted for his great strength. One of these accounts has Schlegel stopping at an inn in the area and asking the bartender for a drink. A bystander, looking for a fight, snatched the glass of liquor away from Schlegel. After ordering a second drink, the same thing happened wherupon our hero said, "Gib mir nach eins" (give me one more). When the bystander made a grab for that as well, Schlegel supposedly grabbed the culprit by his chest and the seat of his trousers and threw him bodily out the window. Turning to the bartender he offered to pay for the drinks and the window. "Never mind," said the innkeeper, "glad to get rid of the fellow." A number of similar stories about this man exist.

Joseph Zehr, son of Dr. Zehr, was nicknamed "pilla Zepp" (Zepp being the German short form of Joseph). The "pilla" prefix grew out of the fact that he made and sold pills which his father had used in his medical practice. However, not being a licensed medical practitioner, Joseph got into trouble over his activities. Apparently the authorities occasionally raided his premises to keep him from dispensing pills. But he claimed to be able to tell when the authorities would appear. Whenever in his sleep he would dream of a bull chasing him, he felt he could expect the authorities to appear shortly thereafter.

Of quite different character was George Jutzi, an early settler in Wilmot. The Mennonite Encyclopedia claims he was one of the few Amishmen who ever wrote a book. Born in France, Jutzi migrated to Pennsylvania thence to Ohio, and finally to Ontario. He took up residence on Lot 8, Bleams Road North, early in the past century. He supposedly wrote his book entitled "Ermohnung an seine Hinterbleibenen" (Letter of Exhortation to his Posterity) in 1842. His writings were published in Pennsylvania in 1853. The first 88 pages of his work were written in prose. The next 237 pages were rhymed verse also containing instructions to his children about the proper Christian conduct of life. Jutzi died in 1881.

Probably the most outstanding churchman during this period was Bishop Peter Litwiller, ordained to serve the Wilmot congregation in 1850. He no doubt contributed much to the healing of a division which had occurred a few years previously in that congregation. It so happened that during his lifetime Father Eugene Funcken came to be parish priest of the Roman Catholic church in St. Agatha. Litwiller lived just north of the town, geography thus making the two men neighbors. They also shared a common German European heritage, and apparently were both quite broad-minded gentlemen. Rather than being an obstacle, their religious differences became an opportunity for dialogue. The two were known to frequently engage in religious discussions. Such was the apparent mutual respect between the two that when Bishop Litwiller passed away in 1878 Father Funcken opened the doors of his church and tolled the church bell when the funeral procession passed by. He also wrote a short article for a local newspaper describing the large attendance at the funeral and the virtues of his fellow clergyman.

1-2. Related to the pioneers. Menno and Elizabeth (daughter of Bishop Peter Litwiller) Schultz, Joseph and Anna (daughter of Dr. Zehr) Baechler.

Faith and Congregational Life

3

Beliefs That Matter

What people believe shapes their lives. Beliefs are of course not the only factor determining how people live, or what they consider important, but they do play a significant role in human affairs. This is so even if such beliefs are not always consciously articulated. Nor is it only the Christian or religious person thus influenced. The atheist or the indifferent, as well as materialists and scientists do not escape the influence of their beliefs or presuppositions. If the reader does not agree, he is at least aware of the writer's bias.

The Reformation happened because of differences in beliefs. The Anabaptist movement and the Amish division all happened, at least in part, because of differences in belief. In the basic Christian concepts the Amish are in agreement with other Christians. They are Anabaptists with reference to the Reformation and their fellow Mennonites. The particular beliefs outlined below, while not distinctively Amish, have been given a distinctive emphasis by them. It is impossible to understand the Amish without some knowledge of these beliefs and practices.

The Amish accept the basic Protestant concept of the scriptures as the sole authority for the church, for faith and life. Their understanding and interpretation of the Bible has always been a dominant factor in all of life. Of the Bible, the New Testament is the highest authority, with the life and teaching of Jesus Christ central. This fact is perhaps best illustrated by the prominence given to the Sermon on the Mount in their instruction for church membership. It is further illustrated in their concept of the Christian life as being primarily discipleship.

In one sense this concept of the Christian life is similar to that of the Catholic orders, in that it calls for unreserved obedience to Christ and his teaching. The difference comes in interpreting what that means and how it is to be expressed in the world. The Amish held that total obedience to Christ was meant for all Christians, not just a select few in the church. Rather than trying to literally imitate Christ as did their Catholic friends in the holy orders, they lived in the world, married, raised families, and engaged in the ordinary pursuits of life. But this life meant for them to seek first the Kingdom of God; spiritual concerns were more important than earthly ones and the life to come more important than the present one. To the Amish it was more important to be honest than rich, to serve than be served, to yield to others than insist on one's way.

A second emphasis in Amish belief which has given shape to their whole life is that of humility, humility before God and a correspondingly low concept of man. Part of this emphasis may well be rooted in their medieval and Augustinian concepts inherited through the Catholic church. Be that as it may, the emphasis on humility before God strengthened the emphasis on obedience, trust, and confidence. It also undergirded the attitudes necessary to enable a brother to confess his sin before the entire church, or not to insist on his own rightness in any given situation. Evidence to this effect is illustrated by the reaction to those of their number who joined the Reformed Mennonites, a splinter group arising in Ontario in the 1840s, who held that they were the only true church. While the Amish naturally believed they were right and their church was also a true church they would never claim to be the only ones in this category.

Humility was the motivation behind the emphasis on plain clothes. The Amish never adopted any particular style of clothing as a religious uniform; they simply resisted change in an attempt to overcome pride as evidenced in dress. The same can be said for hair styles. Two elements in dress which distinguish the Amish to this day are the use of hooks and eyes instead of buttons to fasten their clothes and the fact that, though the Amish are required to wear beards, moustaches are taboo. Both of these oddities were a reaction to the military style of the sixteenth century.

In human relationships, and particularly in attitudes to fellow believers, the Amish took seriously the admonition to "think of others as better than yourself." A young man who served as pastor in a congregation of Amish background remarked about the tendency of people in his congregation, when asked to do something, to excuse themselves by suggesting that someone else could do it better. This incident simply illustrates one aspect of humility as emphasized by the Amish. A further illustration relates to the way in which the Amish chose their ministers. All were chosen by the congregation. A young man, or older one, would never aspire to be a minister. Even though a person would feel such a calling, he would never dare express it. This would be certain evidence of pride and disqualify him immediately for that task.

Another important element in Amish belief was that of brotherhood. This concept was more than a sentimental slogan or merely a symbol of spiritual relationship. It was rather a practical expression of Christian love, meaning equality and sharing. It found expression in the lay ministry, in assuming responsibility for the brother in need, as well as in a general bond of friendship which contributed so much, especially in their earlier years of pioneering in this country. Admittedly, some of these characteristics were also, at least partially, cultural. Some of these qualities were learned in the context of home life. Since families tended to be fairly large there was abundant opportunity to learn to share. Fathers and mothers did everything in their power to assist children in starting their own homes, farms or businesses. Children, likewise, after their parents were older, cared for them. For children to put their parents in an institution, unless it was absolutely essential for medical reasons, would have been the greatest disgrace.

Their response to tragedy is widely known. No matter what form misfortune takes, help is always immediately available. Such demonstrations of compassion were not limited to their own people. Brotherhood implied equality, hence the Amish aversion to conspicuous consumption. For instance, when a young lady revealed a flair for fancy clothes or dresses made of expensive cloth, they would say, "die hutt may schwentz im kopp wie ehra vater kie hutt," meaning that her desires and extravagances went beyond her father's ability to afford.

Part of the Amish aversion to higher education can also be explained on this basis. Again, from the beginning, they took the scripture very literally where it says "knowledge puffs up, but love builds up". Perhaps the Amish were naive and failed to realize that their self-effacement tended to lead to a false humility which created attitudes just as unhealthy and "sinful" as the pride they tried so hard to avoid. On the other hand these emphases did play an important part in creating a close-knit and cohesive community life.

Another aspect of Amish tradition had to do with what is known as the occult. This element has often been over-played in popular treatment of the sect. Again the author would consider this element as more of a medieval cultural heritage than a religious one, although it is difficult always to separate the two. In any case it does reflect the fact that the Amish, too, were children of their time. The phases of the moon were noted carefully to determine the right time to plant crops, butcher pigs, dig fence-post holes or do any of a dozen other things. Besides believing in dubious cures for sickness and disease, the Amish practised charming. They wore jewelry, finger and ear rings, etc., for various ailments. On the whole, however, they discouraged such things as fortune-telling, lucky charms, and bad luck signs. Here their faith in God and divine providence won out over supersitition. Also, more cultural than religious were their many wisdom sayings, which reflect keen psychological insight into human nature and relationships.

Congregational Life

The Amish had a strong emphasis on congregational church government. Having their roots in the Anabaptist-Mennonite tradition which attempted to form a church after a strictly New Testament pattern the Amish believed their pattern to be true to the scriptures. A careful study, however, might indicate that they were influenced just as much by their Catholic background.

A typical congregation had a three-fold ministry. A bishop who was the chief administrator; usually two ministers, whose chief duty was to preach; and two deacons, who, besides looking after the needs of the poor, were also responsible for settling differences between brethren in the church. At least they were responsible for the first contact when someone transgressed the rules of the congregation. In many ways all of the ordained men in a congregation served as a church council. It is a general practice among the Amish to choose their ministers from among the deacons, and a bishop was always chosen from the ministers. This system developed into a three-tier hierarchy but also served as a training school for church leadership.

The matter of choosing men for the ministry was usually in charge of the bishops who would invite any member of the congregation to share the name of a brother who they felt was qualified for the position. If more than the required name, or names, were suggested, the final decision was made by using the lot. In this process, all of the men who were nominated were seated in front with a corresponding number of hymn books on a table or the pulpit. One of the bishops had previously slipped a piece of paper into one of the books, or more if more than one man was to be chosen. Then the nominees were asked each to take a book. The bishop would then proceed to examine each book and the man in whose book the lot was found was considered to be God's choice for the ministry. The above procedure was particularly true in choosing deacons. Ministers were usually chosen from among the deacons and a bishop from among the ministers, this eliminated nominations.

Theoretically all decisions relating to church life were made by the congregation. This included setting standards for conduct or disciplining a member who had transgressed. While the bishop in a congregation had considerable authority he would never dare make any decisions or take any action without consulting his fellow ministers and the congregation. This fact is well illustrated by an incident which took place in an Amish congregation in Ontario early in this century. The bishop of this particular congregation was apparently accused of "lording it over his flock." Consequently, two bishops from the United States were asked in to settle the dispute. The bishop involved was deprived of his prerogatives temporarily and two lay brethren in the congregation were appointed to be his spiritual supervisors and to indicate when they felt that he had amended his ways to the extent that he could again serve as bishop.

It was of course not uncommon for the bishop or the ministerial body of a congregation to decide on their own not to present an issue to the congregation if it was too "hot," or if they felt the congregation might not make the "right" decision. On the other hand, there were occasions when one dissenting voice stalled proposed action by the congregational leaders. In the early years issues were rarely decided by a vote. Actions were taken by unanimous consent or at least without an opposing voice. However, this procedure was not without its problems. Although members did not voice objections they were often not in favor of an action or decision. Rather than cause trouble they would remain quiet in the decision-making process. This in turn would lead to half-hearted support or downright ignoring of a "congregational" decision by some people.

The Amish did not baptize their children, although they were brought up in the church. They dressed in the typical Amish dress and usually accompanied parents to worship service. The main exception to the latter was the communion service which was held twice yearly.

Every year after Easter the bishop of a congregation would invite young people who wanted to unite with the church to enter instruction class. Sometimes if there were only a few responses, no class was held that year. Generally speaking, young people would enter instruction class between the ages of 16 and 20. Very few, if any, young people brought up in Amish homes refused to go to instruction class and to join the church. Instruction always began on Pentecost Sunday and lasted through the summer. Baptism would take place in the early fall in time for the newly baptized members to partake of their first communion with the rest of the congregation.

All of the ordained men would meet with those desiring to become members whenever there was a worship service, usually bi-weekly. On the first meeting each person was asked for his "begarung" (reason for coming to instruction class). Young people would answer, **"Mi begarung is dos ir mir eigedenkt seid in eihrum gebate das ich ein austritt machen kenht aus die auriche base welt, un ein eintritt in die auriche Neues Testament, un mit Gott un seine gemeinde ein ewige gebund un frieda machen durch Jessum Christum. Amen."** A free translation reads, "My desire is that you may remember me in your prayers that I might be able to come out of this very evil world and into the New Testament, and may make an eternal covenant and peace with God and his church through Jesus Christ. Amen."

Instruction would consist of an exposition of the 18 articles of the Dortrecht Confession of Faith, the teaching of Jesus, especially the Sermon on the Mount, and such other exhortations as the ministers felt necessary. It was also customary for a person to memorize one of the articles of faith, referred to above, and give it publicly shortly before baptism. Baptisms were always performed in connection with a regular Sunday morning worship service. While the "class" remained in another room the bishop would ask if anyone in the congregation knew of any reason for withholding baptism from any person in the group of applicants. If no objections were given he would ask the congregation for approval to proceed with the service.

With this formality over, the young people in the instruction class were seated on the very front benches and the worship service proceeded as usual. Following the main sermon the bishop would ask all the candidates for baptism to stand while he asked several questions related to their beliefs. After this the whole group was asked to kneel while several more questions were asked eliciting the baptismal vows. When each person had spoken their vows, the bishop, assisted by a deacon, would baptize them while they remained kneeling.

Baptism in the Amish tradition was administered only upon the confession of faith and in the name of the three persons of the Trinity. Pouring was the mode used. At this point the bishop returned to the first one baptized, who was still kneeling, extended his hand, asked him (or her) to arise while he acknowledged him as "a member of the body of Christ, and a brother (or sister) in the church," concluding by giving each one a symbolic kiss (brotherly greeting). The female members of the class were greeted in the same manner by the deacon's wife. Following the singing of an appropriate hymn opportunity was given for the other ministers of the congregation to welcome the new members into the fellowship of the church.

While church membership gave young people the right to participate in all functions of the congregation they were really not expected to do more than behave themselves and thus be a testimony to Christ whom they professed to follow. However, church membership also meant being "in" the social life of the young people of the congregation. Now they could go to the singings, parties, and begin courting. Adult members transferring from a sister congregation were required to bring a letter of recommendation from their former church which was read publicly, whereupon the person involved was requested to show his willingness to be obedient and faithful by standing. The congregation was asked by the same sign to indicate they were willing to accept the person, or persons, involved.

Adults from another denomination applying for membership had to go through a period of instruction and receive baptism on confession of their faith. The only time baptism would not be required was when such a person had been baptized in another denomination as an adult. The Amish respect adult baptism given in any Christian church. However, persons baptized as infants required rebaptism.

As was indicated in the first chapter, a rather rigid church discipline was one of the distinguishing features of the Amish faith and practice. Sins such as fornication, adultery, or stealing were considered automatically to separate a member from the body of Christ. Other sins such as drunkenness, participation in worldly amusements or sports, usually required a public confession before the entire congregation. Those guilty of the "grosser" sins mentioned before could be reinstated, after official excommunication, by publicly confessing on their knees their specific sin. They were then reinstated by the bishop with the approval of the membership.

All such matters were the concern of the entire congregation. Public sins demanded public confession, since such sins were not only sinning against God but also against the brother and therefore required his forgiveness as well. A member of the church who refused to acknowledge his sin or confess it before the brotherhood was placed under the ban. The bishop would announce publicly that such a person was "delivered to satan for the destruction of the flesh, that his spirit may be saved in the day of the Lord Jesus," and that members were to "shun" such a person. This meant no socializing with him (or her) in any way except to entreat him to acknowledge his sin and make things right with the brotherhood. A milder form of discipline consisted of simply denying such person the privilege of partaking of the communion emblems until he conformed to congregational standards.

However, "shunning" included ordinary everyday eating, according to the Amish. While the interpretation of the above scripture was debatable, some modern translations of the passage would give the Amish interpretation greater credibility than has usually been granted. A more serious fault may have been the legalistic application practised by the Amish. The inconsistency engendered by such a practice was one of the reasons for the eventual discontinuance of the practice by the majority of the Amish in Ontario.

Amish Worship

An Amish worship service was non-liturgical in the formal sense of the word, although over the years it acquired a rather rigid, though simple, form. The service invariably began with the singing of several hymns. The Amish did not have musical instruments in their worship services. **The Vorsinger** (song leader) could be any brother in the congregation who had the ability to lead in singing. The song leader, or leaders, were never formally chosen and led the singing while they remained seated in their usual place in the meeting. The second hymn sung was always the "Lobe Lied" (Praise Song, Ausbund, p. 770). The **Ausbund,** as the Amish hymnal was entitled, was probably the oldest Protestant hymnal extant and still in use. The title had reference to excellence in selection.

While the words and sentiments reflected the persecution and suffering of the Anabaptist forefathers, the tunes originated from contemporary folksongs simply fitted to the hymns they wrote. Another traditional explanation was that these tunes were chosen purposely as a camouflage during the early persecution. During this time in Ontario, (and to this day among the Old Order Amish) tunes were sung to the "longsam weis" (slow tunes) for which there have been numerous explanations. Some link these tunes to the Gregorian chant, others to a simple attempt to slow down popular music to give it a more reverent tone. A third explanation suggests that since these tunes were passed along without musical notation, "in uncontrolled group singing each tune was dragged out leading to all kinds of strange ornamentation foreign to the original tune." Possibly a combination of these factors was responsible for slowness of singing.

Following the opening hymns one of the ministers conducted the "anfang," or opening admonitions, followed by a scripture reading, further admonition and prayer while the congregation knelt. The main sermon followed next, at the conclusion of which opportunity was given by the speaker for "Zeugniss," or testimony by the other ministers present. The minister usually also called upon several laymen for testimony. In this practice the Amish were dialogical in their preaching and teaching, providing for lay response, a practice in vogue in many other churches today. In the Amish context this was just another way of making "brotherhood" more than a slogan. After the testimonies there might be closing remarks by the minister who preached, followed by any announcements, which were usually made by the bishop. This was followed by a closing hymn and the benediction.

Before churches — or meeting houses, as the Amish called them — were built, the worship service was always followed with a common meal. Families took turns in having the "Versammlung" (church) at their homes. Extra tables and benches were made precisely for this and hauled from home to home wherever the service was held. The ingredients of this common meal were fairly well standardized to avoid show or embarrassment for those who did not have the means to provide an elaborate meal. While the meal was the responsibility of the household where the service was held, there were always neighbors and relatives to assist. This practice provided opportunity for informal fellowship among all members of the brotherhood. Worship services were held every other week. The alternate Sundays were given to relaxation or visiting relatives and friends.

The communion service or "grossgemee," also at times called "Abendmahl" or "Nachtmahl," was held twice yearly, at Easter time and in the fall of the year. These services were always preceded by "attnungsgemee," a preparatory service usually held two weeks before the communion service, and a day of prayer and fasting the Sunday immediately preceding the Lord's Supper. At Easter this day of fasting and prayer was held on Good Friday. The preparatory service followed the typical worship service pattern. However the "Anfang," or first part of the service always included reading of Matthew 18 and a homily on humility, warnings against offense, and admonition to reconciliation, forgiveness, and unity. The main sermon elaborated on Christian conduct, warned against the worldly trends and sins in the church and called for obedience to the Amish "Ordnung," or charter as it has sometimes been called.

Following the sermon all the ordained men took turns in testifying to the Word of God as preached. They concluded by acknowledging their own humanness and asking for forbearance and forgiveness should they or members of their families have been an offense to anyone. Next, members were given an opportunity to express their agreement, or disagreement, with the teaching and administration of the church. This was done by the ministers going up and down each row of worshippers and asking for an expression of peace with God and with the brotherhood. If anyone had a grievance he wanted to express, or if he was unsatisfied with the way the ministers handled the affairs of the congregation, he had the privilege of saying so. On rare occasions the communion service had to be postponed until a matter was straightened out. The day of fasting and prayer consisted of abstaining from all food at breakfast and spending the forenoon in reading, meditation on the suffering of Christ, and penitence in order to become a worthy partaker of the sacred emblems of the communion service.

One of the distinguishing features of both the preparatory and communion services was that they usually lasted well into the afternoon. Another was the fact that the children were usually left at home, sometimes with the children of another family or with neighbours or relatives. These were usually "great times" eagerly anticipated by the younger children.

Two sermons always dominated the communion worship service. The first one was on "salvation history" which began with the book of Genesis, the story of man's creation, fall, and God's promise of redemption. The story of redemption was then traced through the patriarchs and the history of Israel to the time of Christ. Secondly the bishop would recount in minute detail the last days of Christ's life and consequent suffering, and then immediately preceding the communion service proper, would expound on the significance of the broken bread and the wine. Then while he read the account of the institution of the Lord's Supper from the scriptures the deacons would place the bread and wine on the table or pulpit in front of the congregation.

After the bishop was through reading he would take a slice of bread (ordinary home-baked bread was used) and ask the congregation to rise while he offered a prayer of thanksgiving and asked God's blessing on the elements. Breaking a small piece of bread from the slice, the bishop would first take a piece himself and then give some to each of the ordained men. He would then give several slices to each minister who would assist him in distributing the same to the members, who remained in their seats. However, as the minister would approach, each row of worshippers would stand to receive the elements.

In the early days it was customary for persons to genuflect as they received the bread. This practice was no doubt carried over from their Catholic background. The same procedure was followed with the wine. The common cup was used, although several cups were usually employed in the larger congregations. Communion was a solemn service emphasizing the suffering of Christ. Again this emphasis no doubt was due in part at least to a common Catholic background, but also to persecution and suffering of the forefathers during the Reformation. In this respect they could identify with the suffering of Christ.

The communion service was followed by the ordinance of foot-washing. After a prayer of thanksgiving, one of the ministers would read the account of Christ washing his disciples' feet and make some comments on the passage. Following this the women would retire to a separate room and all would prepare to wash each other's feet literally. Two persons, having washed each other's feet, would shake hands, greet each other with a kiss, and wish each other the Lord's blessing. The service would then be concluded in the usual manner. The foot-washing service was of special significance to the Amish in light of their concept of brotherhood, humility and a servant-stance toward others.

The occasion of death provided another opportunity for concrete expression of brotherhood. In the event of death or illness, relatives and neighbors were always near to lend assistance in any way needed. After death had occurred they would assume the responsibility of family chores as well as planning for the funeral itself. Until well into the present century the Amish in Ontario had their own people who prepared the body of the deceased and made the necessary arrangements for burial.

The funeral services generally followed the typical Amish pattern. They were always held in the forenoon, with the interment usually preceding the worship service. Following the service almost everyone stayed for the fellowship meal. This often meant feeding several hundred people. On the occasion of the writer's grandfather's funeral, over 700 people stayed for this part of the memorial service. Such occasions did not, however, provide a hardship for the bereaved family. Practically all of the work involved the church community, which provided much of the food as well. Generally the assistance lasted beyond the funeral, depending, of course, on the circumstances. This kind of family caring and sharing during times of bereavement did much to overcome the "sting of death."

Weddings did not usually include the entire community as did the funerals, except perhaps in the early days when the settlement was quite small, although an oncoming marriage was always of special interest to an entire congregation. Every attempt was made by young people to keep their courtship a secret. However, news about young people "going steady" could not be kept secret very long.

Amish young people never secured a marriage license. They would have the banns published two weeks prior to the proposed wedding. Any member of a household unable to attend a worship service in the fall or winter, when most marriages took place, was sure to enquire whether there were any "neuichkeita" (news) from church, meaning, was a proposed marriage announced. A couple would usually absent themselves from the worship service on the Sunday their wedding was announced, spending the day at the girl's home. The following two weeks would be spent preparing for the wedding. The first duty of the young couple would be to visit all the uncles and aunts and extend a personal invitation to the wedding.

Until after the turn of the century the wedding service was always held in the forenoon, sometimes in a regular Sunday morning worship service. Usually also in the home of a neighbor of the bride, since the bride's home had to be readied for the reception. Regardless of when the service was held it followed the traditional Amish pattern. One of the distinguishing features of a wedding sermon was its reference to the story of Tobias and Sara as found in the book of Tobit in the Old Testament Apocrypha. The bridal party was seated in front of the congregation, the men and women facing each other. They would rise and stand together for the marriage vows. The clothing worn for such an occasion was the typical Amish garb. Following the ceremony there was time for testimony by other ministers present. Such testimonies usually consisted of admonition for the young couple and a wish for God's blessing on their lives together.

The wedding reception began with the noon meal. The main table was usually set up in the living room and along the walls in the shape of an L or U. The bride and groom would be seated in the "eck" (corner), with the attendants next, followed by the uncles and aunts of the bride and groom. The young people and children would usually eat in another room. While there were no flowers or flower girls at an Amish wedding, usually two or three younger sisters, or nieces of the bride carried the wedding wine to the table. The bottles usually had a red ribbon tied around the neck making them very attractive. Wine was always served at weddings. Precedent for this was found in the scriptural story of Jesus making wine for a wedding feast as recorded in the Gospel according to St. John. At the conclusion of the meal there would be a time of hymn singing. The hymn book used for this occasion was not the **"Ausbund"** but a smaller book, **"Unparteiiscle Liedersammlung"** (nondenominational church hymns), used generally for evening hymn-sings by the young people. The faster tunes were also used with this hymnal.

The evening meal followed basically the same pattern with one exception. This time the older folks would eat in another room and the young people would eat at the main wedding table. The bride and groom would of course again occupy the "corner" of the table with their attendants. From there on couples would vie with each other in an attempt to get as close to the bridal party as possible. No young people of courting age were allowed to the table without partners. It was almost a disgrace for a young man not to have asked a girl to sit with him. In fact the very shy were often rounded up and "partnered off" to fill the wedding table if there were not enough volunteers.

Following the meal and the usual hymn-sing the young folk would retire to the upstairs rooms. While the older folks usually went home soon after the evening meal the young people would usually stay till after a midnight lunch. They would spend their time visiting and singing both traditional and popular secular music, and sometimes playing games. It was not unusual for the celebrations to continue into the next day for those closest to the bride and groom as well as those assisting with clean-up.

During these early years there was no honeymoon in the modern sense. The young couple would usually live at the bride's home for a time, or go visiting relatives, especially if there were those who could not attend the wedding. Although marriage may have lacked many of the outward romantic elements in current practice in our society, it was a time for community celebration and sharing. The writer's maternal grandmother referred to her wedding day as "the happiest day in my life!"

An important aspect of Amish worship is fellowship. Regardless of the occasion for a worship service, including funerals and weddings — excepting only communion — everybody went including children and babies. Worship consisted of participating together rather than an individualistic communion with God. It was just as important to be on talking terms with one's brother as with God. In other words, Amish worship was characterized by fellowship rather than reverence, by practical admonition rather than inspiration. This does not mean the Amish have little reverence for God, but that reverence was not so much expressed in worship as it was in obedience to his Word in the practical affairs of life. In this sense their worship reflected their theology as much as did their emphasis on practical Christianity.

The Church And the World

4

A Separate Society

From the earliest times the church's relation to the world has been a problem with which Christians have struggled. The New Testament indicates a certain acceptance of the present world and its institutions and on the other hand warns against its allurements. Church history illustrates various stances which the church has taken in the past as well as some of the consequences of such stands. Medieval times probably illustrate the most complete fusion of church and the world. The Reformation brought this issue to a new focus.

Anabaptist understanding led to a radical separation of the church and the world. This meant first of all separation of church and state. The Anabaptists were not against the state as such. They recognized it as a God-ordained institution to which the Christian owed obedience as long as it operated within its own sphere. However, they were against the state being allied with the church or attempting to legislate in spiritual matters. This concept the Amish have maintained, which helps to explain their aversion to political involvement.

The emphasis of separation was also applied to society in general. The Anabaptists did not accept the idea that

Europe was Christian simply because every person was a baptized member of the church. To be Christian meant a radical commitment to live in accord with the teaching of Christ and the entire New Testament. Only those so committed were considered true Christians. This meant that the church derived the norms, values, and guidelines for its life from the scriptures and not from society around it. Both society and the state were considered to be under the domination of the forces of evil. The treatment the Anabaptists received at the hands of both, including the state churches, greatly strengthened that conviction. It is this interpretation and consequent stance which explains, at least in part, the existence of the Amish today.

The Amish applied this concept of separation to the church itself, thus developing their own doctrine of nonconformity. While this is not a unique emphasis of the Amish it acquired a distinctive expression through them. It affected their value system as it pertained to material things. Status symbols were frowned on and frequently became a matter of church discipline. It also greatly influenced the Amish moral and ethical sensitivities. Because of this emphasis on nonconformity almost everything new that came into society in general was considered to be wrong for the Christian. Thus in Amish society ethical values were ascribed to many things and actions which society in general considered completely amoral. The Amish resistance to change can largely be explained on this basis.

On the other hand many people cannot understand, in light of the foregoing, why the Amish could engage in such "worldly" indulgences as smoking or drinking alcoholic beverages. That they did so is probably best explained by recognizing the strong influence of tradition in Amish society. It so happens that the use of liquor and tobacco were part of the cultural milieu out of which our forefathers came. In fact, as we shall see later, when emphasis was placed on smoking and drinking as "evils" many Amish vehemently opposed this new interpretation on a scriptural basis.

Tradition plays a vital role in Amish society in many other ways. Very basic to the literature found in an Amish home is a copy of the **Martyrs Mirror.** This is a large volume of over 1,000 pages, first published in Holland in 1660. Part I of this book contains the stories of those martyred from the time of Christ to the Reformation. The second part gives accounts of many of the martyrs, mostly Anabaptist, of the post-Reformation era. This book is probably the most important and most read book in Amish homes outside of the Bible. A strong sense of being linked with such a multitude of faithful followers of Christ, going back to the Apostles themselves, has played a significant role in maintaining the Amish faith and practices.

Tradition, as well as culture, has decreed also that the elder rather than the younger, the conservative and not the more liberal, should have the most say in matters related to the church. Consequently it has not been too difficult to maintain the "faith of the fathers," at least outwardly, and to keep change to a minimum. Some Amish leaders would readily admit that not all changes which they have rejected were necessarily wrong in themselves. However, the problem lay in knowing where to stop once you went down that road of reasoning. The Old Order Amish of today can point with authority to their more liberal brethren as ample proof of the validity of their fears.

Conflict With the World

The sharp distinction the Anabaptists made between the church and the world, was, as indicated, accentuated by their persecution experience. Some of these conflicts with the world were greatly reduced when the Amish came to Canada. The favorable treatment they received from the Canadian government, and the cordial relationships they experienced with their Catholic, Lutheran, and other Protestant neighbors did much to soften their attitude to the world. However, the conflict remained, though focused on lesser issues, at least for a time. By lesser issues are meant cultural changes which heightened the inner conflict in Amish society.

Before 1870 there were few cultural changes. Until this time new immigrants were still arriving and common European-German culture prevailed in the areas settled by the forefathers. There were, of course, some changes from the very primitive pioneer days. Log cabins had to a large extent been replaced by frame, field-stone, or even brick houses. Fireplaces for heating and cooking had been superceded by iron stoves. In agriculture such new inventions as the threshing machine and even reapers and grain binders had made their appearance. The rather heavy crude wagons had been supplemented by the lighter and more graceful carriages and buggies for general travel. Styles of dress in general had not changed very much and while the Amish avoided the more fancy elements in contemporary clothes their basic styles did not differ greatly from those in common use.

However, all this began to change in the next 50 years. Buggies soon came with solid rubber tires which caused an Amishman to say, half seriously and partly in jest, "yetz commt der dyfel noch in schloppa schoe," (now the devil comes around in bedroom slippers). The rubber-tired carriage was followed by the "horseless carriage," the automobile. In agriculture, technology continued to make life easier with such inventions as the steam engine, replacing the old horse-power for threshing and grinding grain. Of course water wheels and turbines had been used previously to harness the water-power available to saw logs into lumber, grind grain, and do a host of other jobs. An early industrialist in Baden, Jacob Beck, had invented a turbine waterwheel which was used widely in the latter half of the nineteenth century. One of these has recently (1970) been restored and is being used to pump water from a nearby creek to a fish pond in the lawn of the Hondrich homestead south of Baden. An entirely new source of power became available after the turn of the century in the form of hydro-electric power. One of Baden's most famous sons, Sir Adam Beck, son of Jacob mentioned above, was instrumental in spearheading the formation of Ontario Hydro Electric Power Commission. It was during this time that fashions in clothing and grooming began to change markedly. Beards went out of fashion for men, and a little later short hair came in for women. Women's traditional headgear became more fancy and skirts became shorter. Men also wore their hair much shorter and "shingled" haircuts became popular. It was in this area of grooming and dress that the Amish came into serious conflict with the world. This response was natural in light of Jacob Amman's emphasis from the beginning of the movement, the Amish aversion to change, the doctrine of nonconformity and separation from the world, and the importance placed on humility, which precluded any evidence of pride in personal attire. The wearing of caps instead of felt hats in the winter, or the **belzrock** (heavy fur coats), became matters of tension and even church discipline.

The wearing of beards by young married men and shingled hair curts by the unmarried also caused problems. Two young men in the East Zorra congregation decided to get shingled haircuts despite the church's position. Between them they planned what they would say when approached by the ministers of the church. In this case the bishop of the congregation,

Jacob M. Bender, went to talk to the two young offenders. He approached each one separately, however. When the two met later one of them asked the other rather sheepishly, "Well, what did you say to the bishop?" Both admitted that the bishop's kindly approach and earnest rebuke had melted them to tears and had elicited a promise to let their hair grow longer.

Although the women continued to dress very much in traditional styles, changes did begin to make their appearance. The aprons began to disappear, except in worship services, council meetings, communion services, and weddings where the traditional garb was required. The wearing of veils over top of the caps was discontinued. Also during this time the younger women began to wear coats instead of shawls in the colder weather. As indicated earlier, prior to this period the Amish did not dress much differently from other people but now they could be more easily recognized by their out-dated and "plain" clothes.

Another area in which the Amish had conflicts with the world was in the excessive use of alcoholic beverages. The story is told of an Amish farmer who asked his neighbor to look down his throat. When the neighbor replied that he saw nothing unusual, the first man replied, "That's funny, there ought to be a few stumps visible; a whole farm drained down there." It is perhaps not insignificant that a descendant of this particular family left the Amish and joined a Mennonite reform movement around the middle of the nineteenth century.

Another area of conflict in the earlier days was the attitude toward fire insurance. Two insurance policies dating back to the early part of the 1800s have been found among the Amish of Ontario. One of these belonged to a minister of the church, Christian Steinman, who had taken out fire insurance on his buildings in the 1840s. Apparently later on this became a point of tension in the brotherhood. The issue was resolved, at least outwardly, when the Amish organized their own fire insurance aid union. While only two such policies have been discovered it is fairly obvious from an old document that the practice of buying fire insurance from commercial companies was quite common.

The Amish also had some conflicts because some of them became modestly well-to-do and quite progressive in their farming practices. Typical was Christian Wagler, a Wilmot farmer who became a partner in a group interested in importing purebred holstein cattle into the area. Due to opposition from the brotherhood Wagler became the "silent partner" in the company. Another Amish farmer was widely known as an importer and breeder of purebred horses, swine, and poultry. This bit of information was gleaned from some newspaper articles and a personal business card found in Jacob Steinman's personal records. Although the Amish frown upon laziness or slovenliness in work or business, being too progressive is just as unacceptable. This was especially true in relation to conspicuous consumption. One Amish farmer who got the nickname, "cash Zehr," because he always paid cash and made it quite evident that he had a lot of it, finally left the country. He apparently borrowed money extensively for some time to cover his spending. To avail oneself of bankruptcy laws would be condemned by the church but even more obnoxious was his "show of wealth," hence his departure to the U.S.A.

Yet another conflict with the "world" is illustrated by the Amish opposition to the Sunday school. The Sunday school was "worldly" because it was something new and because it was adopted previously by other "worldly" churches. When an Amishman in the Wellesley congregation began conducting a Sunday school in his home in the 1880s, the opposition became so severe that he was forced to discontinue despite an excellent attendance. Although the Amish attitude toward other denominations was quite tolerant, most other churches were considered worldly because they did not practice the simplicity in dress and other areas that the Amish did.

Areas of Accommodation

Despite opposition to change and the resulting conflicts with the world, and in the brotherhood, the Amish did make some changes. In some areas change came easier than in others. Some came about by default rather than conscious effort. This was particularly true of the radio. The radio was unacceptable primarily because it was considered an instrument of entertainment which brought the "world" right into the home. An early Amish businessman in Baden could not convince the church that he needed one to keep abreast of markets and business trends. He was censored by the church for owning a radio despite the fact that he was a Sunday school superintendent. Despite official resistance and even a conference ruling against radios, they gradually came into use and ten years later were quite common with no more church sanctions against them.

The area of greatest accommodation was in the acceptance of technological change. Amish farmers were often some of the first people to purchase new inventions in agricultural technology. New tillage and harvesting equipment, new sources of power, whether steam, gasoline, or electric were readily accepted. A classic example was Abraham Gingerich who farmed just south of Baden. For years a spring-fed pond on his farm had been used to grind grain by the use of a turbine-type water wheel. After the turn of the century when hydro electric power came to Baden, although not yet to the rural community, Gingerich, perhaps inspired by his illustrious neighbour, Sir Adam Beck, bought a dynamo which he powered with his turbine water wheel to produce his own electricity. Later a second as well as a larger upright water wheel were built to enable Gingerich to have sufficient power to operate several electric motors. From 1912-1927, when electricity became commercially available in the community, Gingerich had his own private source of hydro-electric power.

In the area of transportation the Amish also accepted change fairly readily. There was some opposition to top-buggies and rubber-tired buggies at first, but soon after the turn of the century even automobiles were accepted without serious opposition. There was some objection to the telephone when it first made its appearance although this was apparently short-lived. Gasoline-powered farm tractors and all other power machinery was accepted from the beginning by the majority of the Amish in Canada.

Reference was made previously that at least some of the Amish had accepted fire insurance early in the past century. The opposition to insurance sprang from two considerations according to the preamble to the Amish Fire and Storm Aid Union. Insurance was contrary to faith and trust in God for the necessities of life as taught by Jesus, and it meant being unequally yoked with unbelievers in a worldly organization contrary to the apostle Paul's admonition to the Corinthian church. Although against insurance, the church recognized the biblical teaching of mutual sharing and burden bearing. In an attempt to practise their beliefs in this area a concerned group in the Amish community in Ontario organized the Amish Fire and Storm Aid Union.

A number of stories relative to the beginning of this organization have been handed down. One suggests that the idea had its inception with an experience of two Amishmen, Jacob Roth and John Sommers, who both lived in East Zorra

Township. The two men had been in Wilmot and were walking home when a severe thunderstorm struck. Philosophizing on their experience one of the men supposedly asked the other, "If lightning struck your buildings and they burned to the ground, could you rebuild?" The other man confessed he would not, whereupon the two covenanted together to help each other should such a disaster strike.

While this story may indeed be true it is questionable if it had too much to do with the actual formation of the Fire and Storm Aid Union organized in 1872. The Mennonite Conference of Ontario had organized such a union about six years earlier, which may also have been a factor in the establishment of a similar organization by the Amish. How much both groups were influenced by the formation in 1863 of the Waterloo Mutural Fire Insurance Company is difficult to tell, although it is probably more than a coincidence that all three had their beginning within a decade.

Another story relating to the beginning of the Fire and Storm Aid Union has Nicklaus Ruby from East Zorra walking to Elma Township, about 30 miles distant, to discuss with Joseph Steckley the formation of such a plan. This supposedly happened in the month of June, 1872, with the organization effected later the same year. Ruby's concern was that the brotherhood had a responsibility to assist those who had the misfortune of suffering the loss of buildings or crops, especially the poorer members and younger people just starting to farm. There was some opposition and the Union had a slow beginning. There were accusations that the whole thing was just a money-making scheme, that some people wanted to "live like Kings." Reports indicate that there were only about 20 participants in the beginning; this number soon rose to 40 and has continued to increase over the years. Currently (1972) there are about 1,400 participants with the Aid Union carrying a liability of over $40 million.

The Fire and Storm Aid Union is literally just that. It is a very simple arrangement whereby members help each other in event of a disaster. In the early years no money or fees were collected unless there was a need. Sometimes the Union borrowed money to dispense until a rate-bill could be issued to collect funds to cover damages. The organization consists of a directorate composed of one representative from each congregation. The directors in turn organize themselves by appointing a chairman and secretary-treasurer. An annual directors' meeting is held the second Saturday of June. The directors meet in the forenoon to take care of any house-keeping chores and prepare for the annual ratepayers' meeting which follows in the afternoon. The chairman for the ratepayers' meeting is chosen by the meeting itself and is usually someone other than the chairman of the Board of Directors. The directors may bring suggestions or recommendations to the annual meeting for discussion and action, although this is also the privilege of any member.

In more recent times the organization has encountered a number of problems. One of these related to government financing for agriculture. Young people seeking mortgage loans through Junior Farmers were required to carry commercial fire insurance because government officials were not satisfied that the Fire and Storm Aid Union with so little in cash assets was trustworthy. However, after some inquiries and registration of the organization, which has no charter, the government has since honored the organization's policies. A number of internal problems have arisen in past years due to the differences between the Old Order Amish and the larger group. The first of these had to do with insuring tractors. Since the Old Order brethren did not have these, the problem was solved by keeping a separate "power-unit book" in which all tractors insured were recorded, and in case of loss, a separate levy made only on those members who owned tractors. This is now no longer necessary, since most of the Old Order people have themselves acquired tractors.

A second problem was that of insuring church buildings. It usually took a number of annual meeting discussions to solve such an issue. This one was well on its way to solution when the chairman of the Union, Harold Carter, himself an Old Order member, remarked that since they meet in homes and barns, which are insured, he thought it only fair that meeting houses (church buildings) also be insured.

During some of these changes there were some Old Order brethren who felt they should withdraw from the larger organization and establish their own. However, probably largely through the efforts of Carter, this never occurred and the organization remains intact today despite the congregational divisions and wide variety of practices among the Amish in Ontario. There have been numerous other changes and improvements over the last number of years. Many of these have been the result of the vision, patience, and skilful leadership of Harold Carter who also served as chairman for many years.

Besides more adequate records the Union now does maintain a larger cash reserve. For a number of years an annual rate-bill has been issued for the express purpose of accumulating substantial reserve. The current reserve, invested mainly in short-term loans, amounts to approximately $150,000. Ordinarily the practice has been to keep only a very small amount in the bank and to issue a rate-bill only to replenish the account as called for by payment to patrons. Current rate at which participants are charged is usually $2.00 per thousand insured. Annual report of the organization issued in 1969 indicated that the average rate charged over the last 54 years amounts to $1.51 per thousand insured.

More significant than the finances involved over the past 100 years, or the monetary viability of the organization, was the vision and effort of those responsible for inaugurating the plan, and the leadership which has successfully guided it to date. That it continues to serve the entire Amish community from the most progressive to the most conservative Old Order groups is an unparalleled phenomenon in North American Mennonitsm.

The Amish in Ontario held their worship services in their homes and barns till the 1880s. A slight accommodation was made around 1859 when the Wilmot and East Zorra congregations cooperated in building a log cabin across the road from an early joint cemetery on the corner of the 19th Line and the Townline between Perth and Oxford Counties. The building served primarily as a shelter from bad weather in connection with graveside services. The funeral service proper was always held in the home of the deceased person.

A similar building, although larger and of frame construction with a wood floor, was erected by the Wellesley congregation in 1867. This building was also located on the church's cemetery plot and used in connection with funerals. These funeral chapels, although not then so called, were apparently a stepping-stone to the building of church buildings or meeting houses, as the Amish called them. The building in Wellesley was actually used for regular worship services after 1886 when the majority of members in that congregation decided on it. The present Mapleview church is located on the same site.

Although the Amish church as such was slow in accepting the Sunday school, as indicated earlier in this chapter, there were always those among them who accepted innovations more readily. As early as 1860 Amish names appear in the records of a Sunday school conducted by the Evangelical church of Wilmot Centre. Old people in East Zorra and

Wellesley recalled that Amish young people attended Sunday schools conducted in Lutheran churches in their communities. Both of these denominations during this time conducted their services in the German language making it comparatively easy for the Amish to participate. It also substantiates the claim that the Amish were, generally speaking, kindly disposed toward other denominations. Probably not a very large percentage of Amish attended such schools, although the practice seems to have been quite common in areas where such schools existed. This participation no doubt did much to prepare the Amish to accept the Sunday school in their own church later.

As referred to previously, the very first Amish Sunday school was held in Wellesley Township in the home of David Gascho in 1884. Due to opposition the school was discontinued with the result that the Wellesley congregation was the last of the Amish congregations to begin a permanent school in 1912. In the meantime all the other congregations organized Sunday schools. The Hay congregation did so in 1900. Poole congregation had their first session on January 14, 1902. East Zorra followed suit in 1903 and the Wilmot group in 1906.

The early Amish Sunday schools did not use lesson quarterlies but studied directly from the scriptures. For the children and young people it became a German language school. A German A-B-C reading book was used to teach the German language in most congregations till about 1930. Lesson quarterlies were considered a worldly innovation for quite some time. Even though the Amish did not object to having their children taught the English language in the public schools, they were opposed at first to the use of English in their worship services. To use the English in worship was to be worldly and proud. Thus the Sunday school performed a worthy service by teaching the young people the language belonging to the faith of their fathers. This fact also contributed toward the adoption of the church organizations sponsored by the Amish.

The Sunday school made further contributions to accommodation by providing for greater lay participation in the church. It became the channel through which progressive and articulate laymen could share ideas and interpretations of scripture. Inadvertently, even though it started out as a German language school, it ended up being the door through which the English language became acceptable in Amish worship. In this respect the Amish experience with the Sunday school illustrates most graphically how changing times lead to accommodation and accommodation to further change in most unanticipated ways.

3-4. Famous horse breeders among the Amish included Jacob Steinman, Samuel, his son, and Lloyd, his grandson (top). The first businessman at Baden was Noah M. Steinman (below right).

5-6. Self-help and mutual aid. Abraham Gingerich produced his own electricity with power plant (top). Christian Miller serves before dinner drinks at barn-raising (below).

7-9. Clothing styles in first decades of twentieth century. Sisters dressed for school (left), for church (center), and for town (right).

New Congregations And Settlements

5

The Meeting Houses

The changes which came to the Amish worlds on the outside and on the inside were not accepted by all, at least not without some complaint and a great deal of internal dissatisfaction. New styles of clothing and grooming, the increasing use of the English language, and differing approaches to worship eventually led to a serious gap between the more progressive and more conservative elements of the church.

The different convictions with regard to Sunday worship finally resulted in permanent divisions of most of the congregations before the end of the century and, among the worship issues — church music, Sunday school, evening services and meeting houses — the building itself became the most divisive factor.

Presumably the most obvious reason for the erection of meeting houses was a very practical one. The congregations had become too large to continue worship in homes. In most Amish communities this situation was resolved simply by organizing more congregations in order that homes could accommodate the worship service. In light of this fact there must have been other reasons as well for building of meeting houses. The fact that there was considerable opposition to this move, and that some of the Amish continued to worship in homes after meeting houses were built indicates deeper religious aspects to the phenomenon. The opposition may merely have been the typical reaction to something new by a more conservative element.

On the other hand, the fact that the Anabaptist movement grew out of the early reforms of Ulrich Zwingli, who had rejected everything not explicitly taught in the New Testament, may have been behind the rejection of church buildings. In this light, church buildings were a step into the "world" with a resulting temptation to deify a building as "church" — a concept contrary to the Amish emphasis on the church as people. In Amish society there was no sharp dichotomy between the sacred and the secular. Planting and harvesting was as sacred in its way as singing and praying in the typical folk society. Even the majority who were ready for church buildings used the term "meeting house" (**Versammlung haus**) to reinforce the old theology that the church was people.

The congregation in East Zorra Township was the first to move in this direction by building a meeting house in 1883. The building was located on the 16th Line, approximately three miles southeast of Tavistock. The Wilmot congregation erected a building the following year on Lot 18, Snyders Road (Mittlestrasse) about half way between Baden and New Hamburg, on the Steinman homestead. This consequently became known as the Steinman meeting house. The same congregation built another place of worship in 1885 half a mile west of St. Agatha immediately adjacent to a community cemetery and on a plot used previously for a school. Services were held alternately in the two meeting houses.

In the same year (1885) the Hay congregation also built a church building several miles northwest of Zurich on the Bronson Line about half a mile south of the hamlet of Blake. In 1886 the majority of members in the Wellesley congregation decided to conduct their worship services in the "funeral chapel" that had been built in 1867. However, a few families and a deacon, Joseph G. Jantzi, continued to worship in homes. In 1886 the Mornington congregation also built a meeting house just north of the village of Poole. Again, however, two ministers, a deacon, and a number of families continued to worship in homes. Thus in four years all five of the Amish congregations in Ontario had built meeting houses.

The architecture of the Amish further reflected their religious views. Generally, the buildings were devoid of any religious symbolism. Most of the first buildings were of frame construction, with the exception of the Blake church which was a brick building. All were a simple rectangular shape with ordinary roof-pitch and rectangular windows. Usually there were two entrances on the side facing the road, one for the men and the other for the women. Men and women always sat separately in worship services. Invariably there was a porch along the front of the building and sometimes along the side as well.

The two buildings in Wilmot Township were placed with the broadside facing the road and a porch the full length of the three sides plus an extension on the rear of one end on the fourth side for an entry to the rear vestibule. These buildings had three entrances facing the road, one for men, one for women, and another for the front vestibule. The vestibules served the women primarily as clothes closets and mothers' rooms. The rear vestibule also served as a minister's counsel chamber and classroom for the instruction of applicants for church membership. There were no basements under any of these early buildings.

The insides of the churches were typically simple and austere. The walls were plastered and white-washed, the seats usually homemade of pine wood and unpainted. Hat racks were suspended from the ceiling as well as placed on the wall on the men's side. Tables set in the middle of the room along the wall opposite to the main entrance served as pulpits. Behind it was a bench on which would sit all the ministers present facing the congregation. Immediately to either side of the pulpit were the "amen benches" where elderly members sat facing the pulpit. It was from the men's side of these benches that the minister who preached the sermon would ask for testimony (zeugness). This practise once caused an Amish boy to suggest to his father after a service, "Daddy, why don't you sit up there? Then you could say something too."

As a rule there was no raised platform for the pulpit, with the East Zorra church the exception. This church had a slightly raised platform which extended all the way across the front including the amen benches area. The reason for this, offered by some senior members, was to overcome the objections of one minister who vowed not to go behind the pulpit if it were on a raised platform. This way if he entered by the door at the end of the building he was already on the raised part of the floor. And besides, the older people seated on the amen benches shared the same floor level with the ministers.

In addition to the meeting house, sheds were built — usually around three sides of the church — to tie the horses and park the buggies. These sheds also supplied protection from the weather both for horses and carriages. Usually an enclosed section of the horse shed, or a small separate building, served as a wood shed where the janitor could split wood or keep any other equipment he needed. Heating was naturally with the old box-type wood-burning stoves.

Two changes affecting the worship service occurred with the building of meeting houses. From this time on services were held every Sunday instead of bi-weekly as heretofore. Secondly, the traditional fellowship meal following the worship service was discontinued. Otherwise there were no changes in the Amish worship service before the turn of the century.

Divisions in the Church

Although occasional differences and strained relations existed in the Amish community prior to the 1880s, no permanent division had occurred. However, the decision to build meeting houses for worship services caused a permanent schism in the church. While no division due to the meeting house issue as such occurred in the East Zorra, Wilmot and Hay congregations, a number of families in these churches were opposed to the decision. When a year or two later the Wellesley and Mornington congregations also decided to worship in meeting houses (1886), a permanent rift occurred.

It is the author's theory that church splits do not occur in a congregation unless the leaders are involved. Apparently all the ordained men in the other three congregations were in favor of building meeting houses, while in the latter two not all the ordained men were united. In Wellesley only one of the two deacons refused to accept the meeting house idea. In the Mornington congregation two ministers and one deacon were opposed and refused to go along with the innovation. Together with some members they continued to worship in houses. Those families in East Zorra and Wilmot who were not in favor of meeting houses augmented the rather small groups in Wellesley and Mornington Townships who continued to worship in homes.

The above two groups formed the Ontario nucleus of what had by this time received the name "Old Order" in the United States. The "house Amish" as they were also called, in contrast to the "church Amish," functioned as one congregation for a number of years. They held their worship services alternately in Wellesley and Mornington Townships. Since neither of the two groups had a bishop till 1891, bishops from Holmes County, Ohio served communion, had baptisms, and in 1891, ordinations. In Ontario these people were commonly referred to as "Holmsers," because of this connection with the Amish bishops from Holmes County, Ohio.

From 1891 on, when Christian L. Kuepfer from the Mornington Old Order congregation was ordained bishop, the two groups became two independent congregations with Kuepfer serving the Wellesley group for a number of years. In 1902 Peter Jantzi, minister of the Wellesley Old Order congregation, was ordained bishop thus completing the congregational organization of that group as well. For the next 40 years these two congregations continued without change and separate from the others with the exception that they continued to perticipate in the Fire and Storm Aid Union. But we must return to the church Amish now and later talk again about the Old Order congregations.

The Nafziger Congregation

Among the church Amish change continued to come, although slowly and with additional division. One of the major changes in practically all of the congregations was the use of a hymnal other than the **Ausbund** in the worship service. Since quite early, a much smaller hymn book called "**Unparteiische Liedersammlung**" (Nondenominational Song Book) was used by the Amish in their homes and by the young people in their singings. This hymnal was first published in Lancaster, Pennsylvania in 1804. A condensed version with other hymns was published in Berlin (Kitchener), Ontario in 1836 under the title **Gemeinschaftliche Liedersammlung** (Brotherhood Song Book). The one most commonly used by the Amish was published in 1860 under the former title. Since, in comparison, the **Ausbund** was a large thick book, the two were usually referred to as "**das Dünne Buchlein**" (the thin booklet) and "**das dicke Buch**" (the thick book). While the smaller book contained some hymns from the **Ausbund** it also had many newer hymns sung to faster tunes. Exactly when it replaced the **Ausbund** in the worship service is not known; it was without doubt a gradual process. Most of the congregations apparently made this change soon after 1900. It might be said here that the **Ausbund** was replaced completely between 1910-1915 in most congregations as they adopted a new hymnal entitled "**Lieder und Melodien**" (Songs and Melodies). This hymnal featured musical notations for four-part harmony for the first time.

Naturally there was some opposition to **"dem geshtmichagesing"** (four-part harmony) but it was slowly accepted by all the congregations, except the Old Order. Adoption of the hymnal had been preceded by music schools, frequently held in local public schools as evening sessions. Since singing was a prominent part of young people's activities many Amish young people attended these schools. Later these "schools" were held in the Amish meeting houses.

Another significant aspect of the new hymnal was the collection of 457 English hymns, included in the back part of the book without musical notations. The English hymns were at first only used by the young people at their "singings". It is significant that they were included in the regular church hymnal thereby tacitly recognizing the change in language which was slowly taking place. Interestingly, the next hymnal acquired in the 1930s had this order reversed. English hymns with musical notations were in the fore-part of the book and German hymns without the music in the back of the hymnal. But, let us return to the meeting house issue, and related to that the Sunday school.

The Sunday school was introduced in the Hay Township congregation in 1900. In 1902 it was introduced at Mornington, where, in addition to the song book issue, matters relating to dress and some serious personality conflicts resulted in another division. Because of some very unchristian attitudes and action by a few members of the congregation, Bishop Nicholas Nafziger, Minister Peter Spenler, Deacon John Albrecht, and quite a number of members left the congregation and built another meeting house the following year (1904) about a mile west of Poole. This congregation kept the **Ausbund,** did not adopt the Sunday school, and otherwise maintained a more conservative position. We will return to this group in a later chapter.

Division in Hay Township

There apparently were some very early differences in this congregation. The fact that there was no resident bishop after the death in 1850 of John Oesch is evidence of a lack of unity. Bishops from Wilmot and East Zorra served the congregation. From 1915 until the formation of a conference, Bishop Eli Frey from Wauseon, Ohio presided over the congregation. Also in the early years two ministers, Daniel Oesch, son of

Bishop John Oesch, and John D. Bender were censured by the church and apparently they left the church permanently. Cause for this action is not known but indications are that the congregation underwent some serious tensions.

Despite the problems indicated above, the congregations remained a unit till 1908. Early that year Peter Ropp, a Mennonite minister from Pigeon, Michigan, visited in the Blake community. Ropp, originally from Canada and a former Amishman, had moved to Michigan some years earlier and was ordained as minister in a Mennonite congregation there in 1897. The Pigeon, Michigan congregation was under the jurisdiction of the Mennonite Conference of Ontario at this time. Ropp, known as a dynamic preacher, was a son-in-law of John Gascho, minister in the Hay congregation at the time. Consequently, a number of evening meetings were arranged. This marks the first time on record that consecutive evening meetings were held in any of the Amish churches in Ontario. Older members recall how lanterns were set on the window ledges around the church, with a household oil lamp on the pulpit.

Ropp's preaching resulted in quite a number of young people making commitments of faith in Christ. Consequently there were about 19 applicants for church membership the following spring. Problems arose when the young men in the class refused to comply with the traditional Amish dress requirements of wearing the **"Mutze,"** or frock-tail coat as it is sometimes called, and hooks and eyes. As was indicated earlier, this type of "Sunday dress" was a common secular style of coat for men in Europe during the 16th century but had become "sacred" simply because of the Amish resistance to change. Clothing had been an element of dissension in most of the other church splits among the Amish in Ontario. Relative to the incident in the Blake congregation, it is claimed that the parents of the applicants for church membership, rather than the young men themselves, insisted that the young people be baptized without the traditional dress. Complicating the problems was the fact that ordinary coats were worn by the men during the week and even to church on Sunday, but for any special occasion like baptism or marriage the **Mutze** was a requirement.

It was a common practice among Amish congregations that when differences arose a bishop or two from the outside would be invited to come in as mediator. In this case Bishop Eli Frey from Ohio, referred to above, was suggested but was apparently not acceptable to the more conservative element. Finally a request was issued to the Mennonite Conference of Ontario to have bishops from that conference perform the baptisms. Upon mutual agreement between the two sections of the church, 19 persons were baptized and received into the Mennonite church. Approximately 50 additional members from the Blake congregation also transferred their membership to the Mennonite church at this time. There had earlier also been a Mennonite church just south of Zurich but this congregation had ceased to exist before the turn of the century. Now, two years later, in 1910, the new Mennonite congregation built a church building in the town of Zurich, about three miles from the Blake meeting house. The other members of the Hay congregation continued to worship at Blake.

The Lichti Congregation

Several years after the division in Hay Township another church split occurred in the Wellesley congregation. The bishop of this church, Jacob Lichti, was of a more conservative bent of mind. He is credited with making the statement that he wanted to leave the church precisely as he received it. This kind of unbending status quo position was bound to cause trouble when surrounding congregations were yielding to new ideas and new ways of doing things. Up to this point the **Ausbund** hymnal was still being used here, and there was no Sunday school, while in the other Amish congregations in Ontario, with the exception of the Old Order, another hymnal and the Sunday school had been adopted. Actually an attempt had been made in the 1880s to have a Sunday school in this congregation, but it had to be discontinued because of opposition. However, the pressure for change became so great that in 1912 Bishop Lichti and Deacon John Gascho left the congregation and with quite a number of other families formed what came to be known as the Lichti congregation. The group built a meeting house about half a mile east of the older church building. The new group took a similar stance to the Nafziger congregation in Mornington Township. Both congregations remained independent but cooperated over the years.

Let us sum up the changes of this period as they relate to the five original congregations of Wilmot, East Zorra, Hay, Wellesley, and Mornington. The division in both Wellesley and Mornington in the 1880's left us with seven congregations, two of them now called Old Order Amish. Early in the present century another split in the Mornington and Wellesley congregations gave rise to the Nafziger and Lichti churches, bringing the number of Amish congregations to nine. The Nafziger and Lichti congregations took a position about half-way between the Old Order and the original congregations. A fifth split in the Hay congregation resulted in a Mennonite church being formed in Zurich, Ontario, a few miles from the Blake meeting house. This left the total number of Amish congregations in Ontario in 1920 at nine.

Although the Amish have always put strong emphasis on congregational government and local independence, informal sharing among members of the different congregations continued. The ministers would have occasional **"Diener Versammlungen"** (ministers' meetings), which were, however discontinued early in the present century, likely because of the disruptive influence of the divisions detailed above. However, despite the differences and divisions, all nine congregations continued to share in the Fire and Storm Aid Union, organized in 1872 when the community was still "whole". Representatives and interested members continued to meet annually to regulate the affairs of the Union. Thus there remained at least a small, though not insignificant unity in the Amish community.

Attempts at New Settlements

By the middle of the 1870s the five main settlements of Amish in Ontario had been completed, although a few were still arriving from Europe. Occasionally a family or two moved to the United States, but there seems to have been a general lull in emigration till late in the 1880s. Then, for the next 30 years there was considerable emigration of Amish, as well as a few attempts at new settlements in Canada.

There were probably several reasons for the phenomenon. First of all a rather severe economic depression in the eighties and nineties caused some real hardship among the Amish. Secondly, a number of states in the union were just opening up, offering prospects of cheap land and greater opportunities. The Amish were not the only ones leaving for the United States. The difficult economic circumstances in Canada and the allurements of the American frontier caused an "alarming rate" of emigration according to one historian. The writer recalls hearing older people tell stories about utopian conditions across the border, about "roasted pigeons flying right into your mouth," "wonderful big strawberries" in Virginia, and "money so plentiful that women carried it by the apron full".

Although satirical exaggeration with a slightly self-righteous bias, these statements probably indicate part of the reason for migrating. Older people have also confirmed that some left because of the tensions due to change which existed in the church during this time. Congregations had been divided over the meeting house issue and there were frequent disagreements over church **"Ordnung"** (order). Consequently some people left with the hope of setting up more amiable communities. Precise dates for the beginning of each settlement have not been determined. In some cases most of the families settling in one particular area left Ontario together but this was not always true. Quite frequently families who left were blood relations of one degree or another.

Some of the first to leave for Nebraska were the Menno Erb, Valentine Gerber, and Peter Kennel families. These left in 1888 and settled in Holt County in northern Nebraska. Later Peter Kennel was ordained minister and still later bishop of a congregation near Schickley, in the southern part of the state. The Kennels had arrived in Ontario only in 1881, and had been housed and given work by the writer's grandfather. Apparently the early settlement in Holt County disintegrated because in the early nineties the Valentine Gerber family moved to Minnesota where a number of Amish families from Ontario were beginning a new settlement.

The settlement in Minnesota was in the south-western part of the state, around Wilmont, in Nobles County. Besides the Valentine Gerber family were the following: Joseph Gerber, a bishop from the Mornington congregation; the David and Daniel Jantzi families; Moses Schlabachs and Jacob Gaschos. After the turn of the century this settlement disintegrated with Valentine Gerbers, Daniel Jantzis, and Moses Schlabachs coming back to Ontario, while the others settled in Michigan. Apparently the main reason for the non-success of this attempt was the lack of spiritual unity in the group.

Besides the families from Minnesota, quite a number of other Amish families from Ontario settled in Michigan. In this state no one particular settlement of Ontario Amish was established. Peter Ropp, referred to earlier in this chapter as conducting evening meetings in the Blake church, had migrated to Huron County, Michigan where he joined a Mennonite congregation and was ordained in 1897. Michael S. Zehr, a son of Bishop Christian G. Zehr of the Wellesley congregation in Ontario, was ordained in the Pigeon River Amish congregation in Pigeon, Michigan in 1905. Joseph Ramseyer born near New Hamburg, Ontario and later living in Hay Township also migrated to Michigan where he became a member of the Defenceless Mennonite Church and was ordained to the ministry. Ramseyer became a noted evangelist, founder of the Missionary Church Association and for many years president of Fort Wayne Bible College. Other families moving to Michigan after the turn of the century were two Christian Schwartzentruber families, and the families of Joseph and Jacob Albrecht, Joseph Ropp, John Gascho, John Moyer, Jacob Litwiller, and Joseph Schultz.

Also in the 1890s a number of families emigrated to the La Junta area in the state of Colorado. Christian Lichtis, Menno Bosharts, John and Fannie Jantzi, Christian Kuepfers, Menno Schultzes, Nichlaus Schlegels, and Joseph Rubys were some of the families to locate there. Only the Ruby and Schultz families remained. Some of the others later moved to Nebraska, Oregon, and back to Ontario. Christian Kuepfer, for instance, became deathly ill with what apparently was homesickness. Several became penniless due to drought and storms. The storms were so bad, according to Menno Boshart, who came home without the typical Amish beard, that it just "blew his beard away"

Another Amish settlement with three families from Ontario and some others from Maryland was established early in the 1890s in Fraquier County, Virginia. This group, which included the Christian Roth, Michael Wagler and Joseph Kropf families from Ontario was located about halfway between Washington D.C. and the Blue Ridge Mountains, near a village called Bealton. All of the Ontario families returned shortly after 1900. Reasons given were primarily economic. The land was depleted and consequently crops were poor. Two other young men from Ontario, John and Jacob Mayer, who worked in the area for a summer, did not stay. Others could go to Virginia, they said, but it was too hot there as far as they were concerned.

Several other states to which the Amish migrated during this time were Oregon and New York. Moses and Daniel Erbs located in Oregon as did a Jacob Gingerich family from Hay Township. Another Jacob Gingerich from Wilmot Township, as well as a Solomon Jantzi family, moved to New York state.

Two other Canadian settlements occurred after the turn of the century. A number of families moved to the provinces of Saskatchewan and Alberta. Among them were Joseph Nafzigers, Moses Erbs, Michael and Daniel Jantzi families, and the Joseph Leis family. After the death of Michael Jantzi his

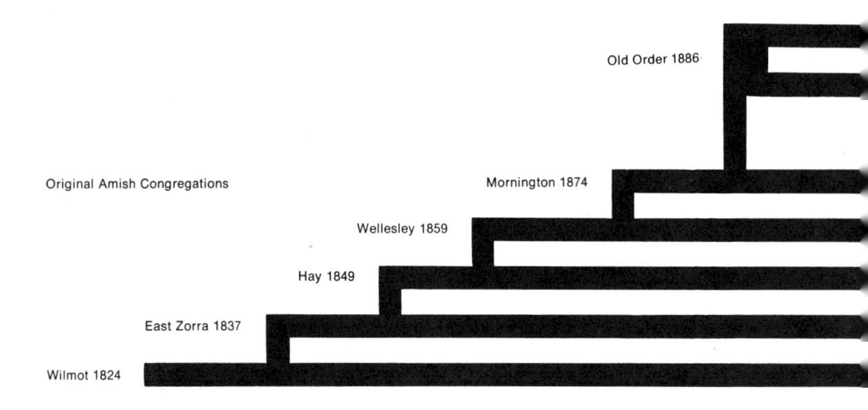
Old Order 1886
Original Amish Congregations
Mornington 1874
Wellesley 1859
Hay 1849
East Zorra 1837
Wilmot 1824

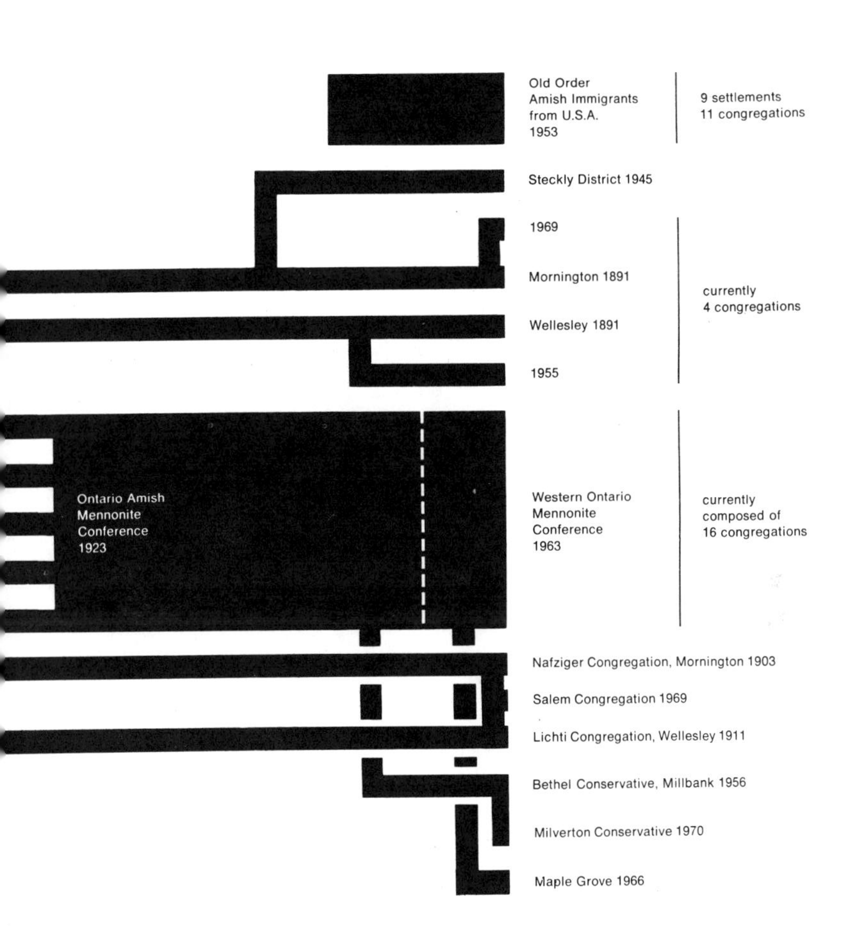

10. The Amish Family Tree.

widow and their children, and the Daniel Jantzis returned to Ontario. The other families remained in the Canadian west, although no Amish congregation was ever formed there. The Amish joined Mennonite or other congregations.

A settlement nearer home in Canboro Township, Haldimand County was begun in 1905. About seven families participated in this venture, primarily from the Wellesley and East Zorra congregations. They were David Gascho, Christian Schwartzentruber, John Schwartzentruber, Daniel K. Jantzi, Michael and Moses Jantzi. Valentine Gerbers, who had just recently returned from Minnesota, also joined the group. Gerber had been ordained a minister while in Nebraska and served the group in this capacity. Bishop Jacob M. Bender from the East Zorra congregation held a baptismal service for the new congregation in 1909. By 1915 all of the members had returned to the home base. The extremely heavy clay soil and the poor quality drinking water were given as reasons for not staying. It was also reported that there was lack of agreement on church matters.

From the facts given above it is evident that the attempts to establish new settlements were not very successful. The depression, which caused the attempts in the first place, was not limited to Canada. Consequently, most of the families came home poorer than they left. Another possible reason for failure was that they were attempting to run away from problems. Most who left because of problems in the home church discovered that they took their problems with them. Probably because of increased economic prosperity, the lessons learned through their migration experiences, and the First World War, no further attempts at new settlements were made for over 40 years.

New Institutions And Programs

6

Some Outside Influences

In the previous chapters we indicated some of the changes which took place just before and after the turn of the century. It is quite obvious that many of these changes came about through corresponding cultural changes in Canadian society. But some changes were peculiar to the Amish community. It is of course impossible to isolate all the factors which contributed to those changes. However, in the writer's view there were a number of influences which gave shape to the new institutions and programs that emerged in the 1920s and beyond.

Revivalism, a predominately American phenomenon dating back to the eighteenth century, did not have any appreciable affect on the Amish until after 1900. For 20 years the influence of revivalism was primarily indirect. The Amish had, however, been influenced by pietism in Europe many years earlier. This is amply illustrated in their devotional literature. Since American revivalism was at least partly an outgrowth of pietism, some of its emphases were not entirely foreign to the Amish. Some of its negative manifestations made for very cautious acceptance. In the mind of the Amish these included: some divisions in the

Mennonite brotherhood in both the United States and Ontario, the new ways, the protracted evening meetings, and the calling for open commitments.

The first such meetings held among the Amish in Ontario were those at Blake, in Hay Township, with Peter Ropp as preacher. This incident, referred to earlier, was at least indirectly the cause of a division in that congregation. No record of any other such meetings before 1920 have been discovered. This type of meeting had by that time become fairly well accepted by the Mennonite churches in the area, and patronized by the Amish to some extent. The people who attended this type of meeting were frequently active also in the Sunday school and in this way exerted considerable influence.

Others were influenced by Pentecostalism and other aggressive groups. A member of the Wilmot congregation, Peter Moyer, having come under such influence, felt called to erect a church building in the town of Baden and did so at his own expense. Moyer's vision included an effort of outreach to the unchurched, hoping to revitalize and unite the Amish and Mennonite churches in the area. However, such an individualistic and uncongregational action was greatly frowned upon by the Amish in particular and exerted little influence among them. The Baden mission, as it came to be called, was built in 1913. It was later administered jointly by the Amish and Mennonites, but since 1945 has been an organized congregation in the Mennonite Conference of Ontario.

Bible Conferences

The Bible conference movement was an outgrowth of the revival movement within the Mennonite church, and was in many ways very similar to the Wesleyan or Methodist Bible Class phenomenon. These conferences began among the Mennonites in Ontario in 1899 and soon gained popularity. The first Bible conference among the Amish was held in the Mornington or Poole congregation in 1911, with E. L. Frey and C. Z. Yoder as instructors. Both of these men were Americans, with Frey having bishop oversight of the Poole congregation. This particular conference had morning and evening sessions Tuesday through Thursday. Themes discussed included biblical ones such as faith, love, life, worship, forgiveness, and resurrection. Of a more practical nature were such topics as worldly gatherings, nonconformity to the world, and mission work.

Whether convictions for missionary service stemmed from the above or some other source matters little. That such convictions were present among the Amish during this time is amply illustrated by the account of a happening in the Wellesley congregation. A rather gifted young man from this church felt called to foreign mission work. His ability and convictions were probably too evident and as a consequence he was severely ostracised by his fellow members. He is reported to have been an excellent song leader but every attempt to exercise his gifts was thwarted because of the strong feeling against the things he stood for. Due largely to this complete rejection by his brethren the young man had a mental breakdown and ended his own life.

While the above is the only Bible conference on record before 1920, some of the Amish were influenced by such events held in the surrounding Mennonite churches. Many of the emphases which grew out of these sessions did not greatly affect the Amish way of life until ten to 20 years later.

World War I

The Amish, like their Mennonite brethren, are pacifists. The term used by them is "nonresistant," with the position they hold going back to the Reformation and the Anabaptist movement. The Canadian government respected their position in World War I and Amish young men were exempt from military service. However, the war did affect the group in a number of ways. For instance, during the war Bishop Eli Frey, who had charge of the Mornington congregation, had considerable difficulty crossing the border and consequently encouraged the formation of a church conference. Before this time there had been no formal organization holding the congregations in Ontario together. Hence when problems arose it was common practice for congregations to ask for assistance from churches or conferences in the United States. Frey encouraged the formation of an Ontario Amish conference to assume responsibility in such circumstances. An attempt to do so failed in 1918 but it did succeed a few years later. Hence the war was, at least in part, responsible for the formation of a conference structure among the Amish in Ontario.

Another result of the war was the closer cooperation of the Amish with related churches. Following the above governmental action, the Amish co-signed a petition to the Government of Canada expressing appreciation for past favors and requesting consideration in the present crisis. Fostered by cooperation on matters related to the war, the same attitude issued in other interaction between the Amish and the Mennonites in Ontario. An Amish minister who played an important role in this area was Jacob R. Bender. In addition to serving as co-signer of the petition mentioned, Bender, with Christian Gascho and Christian Schultz, represented the Amish in the Non-Resistant Relief Organization.

This organization, which included other nonresistant churches in Ontario, was formed during the war "for the purpose of considering ways and means by which the nonresistant bodies which they represent might be able to express in some practical manner their profound gratitude and appreciation for the enjoyment of exemption from every class of military service." The organization was responsible for collecting approximately $75,000 for relief which was distributed to the following agencies: Merchant Sailors' Relief Organization, The Soldiers' Aid Commission of Ontario, The Belgian Relief Fund, and the Canadian-Serbian Relief Committee.

This Inter-Mennonite Committee continued after the war and for many years was an important avenue of service and fellowship among Amish, Mennonite, and other related groups. It can be safely assumed that World War I served to broaden the horizon of the Amish community in Canada making possible their broader cooperation with other groups and their acceptance of new ideas and new ways, especially from their Mennonite brethren. These experiences prepared the Amish for the mission and service opportunities which came their way in the years that followed.

The Sunday School Conference

In one sense the Amish church was very much a lay church. Leadership was chosen directly out of the laity without any formal training for their task. All decisions, at least theoretically, were made by the whole congregation. Twice a year before the communion service every layman had an opportunity, during "Ordnungs Gemee" (council meeting), to express any complaints about congregational leadership or administration. Laymen were given the opportunity to give testimony to the messages brought by the ministers in the regular worship. Despite these opportunities there were usually only a select few who availed themselves of these privileges. It was not uncommon for a few vocal laymen practically to run the church. Frequently it was the more conservative and dogmatic element whose voices were the loudest — and because nobody else wanted to cause trouble — that determined the direction of the church. Since there are exceptions to all rules, the same was true here. The Amish have also had a very strong emphasis on ordination and on submission to the elder or bishop. Consequently, the direction any congregation went was often largely determined by the bishop.

It is in light of these facts that the writer claims the Sunday school provided a unique avenue for greater lay participation. Often the influence by laymen was quite indirect, but nonetheless very real. Some very capable, alert, and well read men were chosen as leaders. Sometimes the leaders of the Sunday school were considerably more capable than the ordained ministers, a fact which often proved rather threatening to the ordained leadership. The writer recalls conversations among older people indicating a real power struggle between church and Sunday school. In a very real sense they were two separate entities. The Sunday school tended to be the avenue through which progressive laymen expressed their views and propagated new ideas. This left the ordained men with the responsibility to maintain peace. Or, if the ordained leadership tended to be more conservative, which it often was, it became the champion of the status quo and was looked upon as the block to progress. Usually, of course, the leadership of neither institution was wholly in one camp or the other. There were some progressive ordained leaders in the church during the early part of this period, although the Sunday school was the "cutting edge" of the church beginning in the 1920s and continuing to the 1940s.

The Mennonites in Ontario had meetings for Sunday school workers as early as 1890. It was 1916, however, before an official Sunday school conference was organized. The Amish conducted their first Sunday school conference May 24-25, 1922. That was a year before a church conference uniting the congregations was founded. The first moderator of the Amish Sunday school conference was Bishop Eli L. Frey from Ohio. Frey exerted considerable influence in Ontario for quite some time and was the man largely responsible for beginning a Sunday school conference. He had attempted to have the church leaders form a church conference in 1918, partly because he was refused entry into Canada during the late years of the war. That attempt had, however, not succeeded; apparently a conference to discuss issues related to the Sunday school was less threatening.

Although that conference was related primarily to the Sunday school, every speaker on the program was an ordained minister. Topics treated were these: What is the Object of this Conference, Learning to Trust Each Other, Conditions of Success in Sunday School Work, Qualifications of a Sunday School Superintendent, Teachers' Preparation and Responsibility, Attitude of Sunday School Toward Superintendents, How to Interest Our Young People in Christian Duty and Privileges, The Family Altar, The Value of Memorizing the Bible, Effective and Defective Teaching, Punctuality, Our Responsibility Toward the Child, The Value and Power of Song in Sunday School Work, The Sunday School Worker's Reward. The final session included a "Question drawer" and was concluded with a sermon by the moderator. The conference met annually after this until 1957 when it was superceded by a new organization called Christian Nurture Council.

In the years that followed the first Sunday school conference the event usually took place the first or second weekend in September, alternating with a similar meeting by the Mennonites in Ontario. Until near the end in 1957 it was the most popular and best attended meeting of the Amish in Ontario. The greatest problem was to accommodate the crowds. At times large tents were rented. After church buildings were enlarged these were again used with outside loud speaker systems for those not able to get in. On various occasions the possibilities of erecting a large conference building were discussed but this never became a reality. In the 1950s the annual meetings were usually held in community buildings in New Hamburg, Milverton, or Stratford.

In addition to the regular program for adults, a children's meeting, always well attended, was held in connection with this event. In later years a special informal and usually outdoor service was planned for those staying on the grounds over the supper hour on Sundays. This service was called a "sun-set meeting" and consisted primarily of testimonies, sharing of experiences in Sunday school work, and a brief inspirational message.

Although the early Sunday school conference meetings were dominated by the clergy this slowly changed as more laymen were invited to speak on various topics. However, only ordained men were chosen to constitute the executive committee. Sunday school superintendents participated in choosing the members of the executive as well as in making decisions on guest speakers and other matters related to the annual meeting.

The Sunday school conference was also the organization through which the Amish in Ontario first began participating in the inter-conference organization of the Mennonite churches called Mennonite General Conference. The latter was simply an advisory, cooperative, organization in which all Mennonite and Amish conferences in the United States and Canada were eligible for membership. While the Amish in Ontario did not become actual members of this organization until 1959 they did on occasions send a delegate to the meetings of the Commission for Christian Education, an organization under Mennonite General Conference. Furthermore, the Amish did attend the Ontario Mennonite Sunday school conference, usually held in Kitchener, in sizeable numbers, thus fostering a growing inter-Mennonite relationship on a local level.

The Sunday school itself was a new idea which took a considerable time to gain acceptance among the Amish. Even after its general acceptance, it operated under certain restrictions. All teaching was to be in German, including instruction in German reading for the children. Secondly, instruction was to be strictly from the Bible itself. It was not till the 1920s that "lesson helps" were sanctioned. It took about another ten years before the English language was permitted. However, the use of English in the church did come in through the Sunday school. Not too long afterward, an occasional sermon was preached in English. Thus the door was slowly opening, making possible larger outside influences. On the other hand not all the wider influence or new ideas came into the church this way. Some of the ordained men were of the progressive type, who through reading and wider Mennonite acquaintance and work, were also responsible for an enlarged vision.

Another of the contemporary ideas which met considerable opposition was that of missions — the church's evangelistic task. Even before the Amish division in Europe the original Mennonite evangelistic thrust had been blunted. The Mennonites had become the "quiet in the land". Amish conservatism and emphasis on humility tended to accentuate this trend. The emphasis was placed on living the faith and thus letting one's life quietly give testimony to the gospel.

However, the general awakening among the Mennonites around the turn of the century and following had led to the conviction that the church had a present-day responsibility to evangelize.

Peter Moyer, a member of the Wilmot congregation felt led to build a mission church in the town of Baden in 1913. Soon others felt called to spread the gospel. Moyer encouraged one young man to do his mission work in his home congregation. Later this man served the Wilmot congregation for many years as Sunday school teacher and superintendent. In this way a new sense of mission developed in the Amish church. This will be a later topic of discussion.

A third new idea which came into the church largely through the Sunday school related to the evils of alcoholic beverages and tobacco. Generally speaking, the Amish were not adverse to the use of either in moderation. It was not uncommon for the ordained leadership to use both, although there were exceptions both among the laity and in leadership. It is reported that Dr. Zehr, an early pioneer and minister in the East Zorra congregation, was opposed to the use of tobacco, referring to it as a "yunge ongewonheide un a alte saweri," meaning essentially that the use of tobacco was a "habit one formed while young which was really an old mess". As a reaction against the misuse of alcoholic beverages, and through the influence of the revival and holiness movements, total abstinence relative to both was taught. The Uniform Sunday school lessons, with their quarterly "temperance lesson," provided an excellent opportunity to foster this teaching. Severely resisted at first, total abstinence slowly became the more acceptable position, although it has never been totally accepted or practised by the Amish.

The Church Conference

For almost 100 years after the first Amish congregation was organized in 1824 no attempt was made to create a formal structure relating to the congregations. During the early years there was much informal sharing among settlements. With church services conducted only bi-weekly, visiting other settlements and attending worship services there kept the relationships vital. In addition the leaders got together occasionally for "Diener Versammlungen" (ministers' meetings). Since no record was kept of these meetings it is not known how often they were held, when started, or when they were discontinued.

Following the divisions during the meeting house controversy it became popular, it seems, to call on the Amish brotherhood and its bishops in the United States for assistance, oversight, and arbitration. As indicated in an earlier chapter the Old Order congregations were assisted by bishops from Holmes County, Ohio. In 1903, following the Nafziger division in Mornington, Bishop Schlegel from Nebraska and Bishop Gerig from Ohio assisted in ordinations in the Poole congregation since only a deacon remained of the former ministry. From this incident till 1923 this congregation was supervised by a bishop from an American conference known as the Eastern Amish Mennonite Conference. The bishop from this conference who officiated most frequently in Ontario was Eli Frey. He served not only the Poole congregation but also Blake from 1915-1923.

In 1913 Frey and Daniel Y. Johns also became arbitrators in a controversy in the Wilmot congregation. Consequently the bishop of this congregation was deprived of some of his leadership prerogatives until "he has shown forbearance and given evidence of a willingness to work with and promote the welfare of the brotherhood . . ." Two laymen, Samuel Bender and Aaron Gingerich, were chosen as spiritual fathers to Bishop Steinman and asked to indicate when they felt he could again resume full responsibility.

During the closing years of World War I, Frey, on one of his trips to minister to the Poole congregation, was refused entry into Canada, presumably because of his pacifist position. He suggested the congregation ask the bishop of the East Zorra congregation to serve them. In the ensuing discussion it was decided to call a meeting of all the ordained men with the object of forming a conference organization. The attempt failed, however, even though a meeting of the ordained men was held in the East Zorra meeting house on June 27-28, 1918. The Amish emphasis on congregational church government, plus the fear of centralized power, were sufficiently strong to thwart the effort.

No further church-wide meeting was held till 1922 when a Sunday school conference was organized and held in the Wilmot meeting house. Bishop Frey from Ohio served as moderator of this conference for the first year and was probably the person mainly responsible for its formation. He played a similar role in the formation of a church conference the following year. Actions were taken to organize formally and to meet annually. A constitution was adopted two years later — in 1925. Following the conference session in 1923 Bishop Daniel Jutzi of the East Zorra congregation had been chosen as moderator, a position he held till 1937. Bishop Jutzi, together with his fellow-minister, Jacob R. Bender, played a vital role, not only in the formation of the conference, but also in its ongoing program.

While the first attempt to form a conference was related to Frey's inability to enter the country, that was no longer the case in 1923. A hint as to the deeper reason for conference organization can be gleaned from a statement by an earlier historian. Jacob R. Bender writes: "The congregations were standing and working independently, and naturally were drifting further apart." Much of the earlier informal sharing was no longer taking place. The disruptive influence of the divisions in the late nineteenth and early twentieth centuries was no doubt responsible for the discontinuance of the ministers' meetings. The failure to resolve the differences and tensions created by the changing times and needs resulted not only in divisions but in deep personality clashes, suspicions, and distrust which marred the Christian fellowship. Formation of a church conference was one attempt to restore that broader fellowship.

The purpose of the conference was "to consider questions relative to the work of the church, and adopt such measures as shall advance the cause of Christ, and promote the unity and general welfare of the church". In an article in the same document on conference leadership it is further stated, "The conference shall endeavor to lead and unify the churches in upholding such rules and disciplines as are necessary to restrain upon gospel principles, the great modern tendency to worldliness and in promoting spiritual life in the churches." The conference served primarily as an opportunity for sharing and discussing matters of common interest and concern.

Besides an executive committee, a resolutions committee was appointed and functioned beginning with the 1924 session. Early in the thirties a committee was asked to gather and publish in pamphlet form all the questions discussed, together with resolutions, from 1924-1931. This report not only illuminates the issues faced but also indicates that quite a number of other Mennonite leaders frequented the conference sessions. Absent from participation, however, were representatives from the more conservative Amish groups.

Congregationally, conference membership consisted of

the five original congregations: Wilmot, East Zorra, Hay, Wellesley and Mornington. By this time the Mornington congregation was referred to as the Poole church, named after the hamlet of Poole and to differentiate it from the Nafziger and Old Order congregations in the same township. The Wellesley congregation became the Mapleview church to distinguish it from the Lichti or Cedar Grove and Old Order congregations of that area. The congregation in Hay Township was referred to as the Blake church, after the village of Blake, to distinguish it from the Mennonite church in nearby Zurich. East Zorra and Wilmot retained their old names.

Circumstances in the early twenties caused the conference to be concerned with issues beyond itself. A couple from the Wilmot congregation had volunteered for foreign missionary service and was accepted and commissioned to serve in South America by the Mennonite Board of Missions and Charities of Elkhart, Indiana. The year following (1925) another couple from the same congregation was also commissioned to serve in the same country. The Elkhart board invited the conference to support the new missionaries. Consequently a missions committee was appointed at the annual conference in 1925 to collect and dispense funds for the support of the two missionary couples.

In 1932 the conference appointed a Bible school board. After the evangelistic-revival movement had made itself felt in the Mennonite churches in Ontario just before the turn of the century, Bible conferences became popular. These were usually conducted in connection with, or following, revival meetings and lasted several days. Early in this century Bible classes of several weeks were inaugurated, usually during the winter months. Winter Bible schools became popular in the years that followed. The Amish were characteristically slow in accepting this new approach, but finally, through the efforts of Jacob R. Bender and others, the conference approved of them. The new board set up a program of studies, appointed a faculty, and held its first Winter Bible school in the fall of 1932 in the East Zorra church. The following winter an additional school was held in Wilmot. Other congregations followed suit and the Winter Bible school movement flourished for the next 20 years. Still predominantly rural and with few young people attending high school, the winters provided ample spare time for the Amish to attend the Bible school.

Another development in the conference during the thirties

was the beginning of formal inter-Mennonite cooperation. In 1934 both the Mennonite General Conference and its mission board at Elkhart requested the Amish congregations to appoint members to the respective organizations. However, apparently there was insufficient support and both requests were shelved. In 1936 the conference did appoint Jacob R. Bender as a delegate to the meetings of the General Mission Board as well as of the Ontario Mennonite Mission Board. The Amish conference, however, never did pick up the request from General Conference to send a delegate.

There were other indicators of future cooperation. Jacob R. Bender, Christian Gascho, minister of the Steinman congregation, and Christian Schultz from Poole had been members of the Peace Churches' Nonresistant Relief Organization since 1918. Also in 1938, Peter Moyer's dream of getting the Amish and the Mennonites together, when he built his chapel in Baden in 1913, seemed to be coming nearer fulfilment when the Amish conference agreed to cooperate in supplying ministers and jointly administer the program at the Baden mission. All of these projects were small beginnings in the larger cooperation which followed.

Missionaries and Missions

It seems odd that the first Mennonite foreign missionaries to leave Canadian soil for a foreign country were Amish. Generally considered the most conservative of the Mennonite family, it has not been unusual for the most aggressive and gifted leaders to emerge from their numbers. The account of two young Amish couples who left for South America in the 1920s is evidence of this fact.

Amos Schwartzentruber, a descendant of the first Amish family to locate permanently in Wilmot Township in 1823, was a typical young Amishman. He married quite young and settled on his father's farm. However, he experienced a rather severe crisis when his young wife passed away in 1917. Conscious that his own mother had dedicated him to God at birth, Amos felt called to the Lord's work. The following year he left to attend Bible school in Chicago in preparation for mission service. Here he met Edna Litwiller, a young lady from his home community. The two were married and served in the Youngstown mission in Youngstown, Ohio.

After the mission closed, the Schwartzentrubers came back to Ontario and again took up residence on the home farm. In 1923 they volunteered to go to South America and were accepted by the Mennonite Board of Missions and Charities. After considerable correspondence between the board and the Wilmot congregation, Bishop Daniel Steinman finally consented to have Amos ordained to the ministry in the St. Agatha meeting house. The ordination was in charge of Bishop Eli Frey of Ohio. The couple left for South America later the same year (1924).

The second couple, Nelson and Ada Litwiller (Nelson being a brother of Mrs. Schwartzentruber) went to the same country, Argentina, the following year. Nelson was one of the first young Amishmen to attend high school. He tells how he attended political campaign meetings with his father and decided to be a politician. This was changed, however, when toward the close of his high school career he experienced a spiritual conversion. After finishing high school, he entered teachers' college at Stratford, Ontario, after which he taught school to pay off his school debt. To keep peace in the family, his father had written up against him a yearly amount while he attended school. After a brief teaching career and marriage, the Litwillers attended Bethany Seminary in Chicago in further preparation for foreign service. Finally, after receiving a college and seminary degree the Litwillers were commissioned in 1925 to go to South America.

Both couples have acknowledged the place of wider influences in their early years as playing an important part in shaping their lives. One of these was the revival movement sweeping through the Mennonite church beginning before the turn of the century. The other was the influence of returned missionaries from India (the first Mennonite foreign mission field) and Africa, through Allan Schultz (of Amish background), and also some Missionary Alliance people of Mennonite background. However, some influence and encouragement also came from Amish sources. Litwiller experienced his sense of call to foreign work at a meeting in the Baden mission. In addition, before either Litwiller or Schwartzentruber left the community they received quite a few votes when nominations were held for deacons in the Wilmot congregation. This was fairly concrete evidence that the two young men had considerable support in their home church. The bishops in charge disqualified the two because they were not married. Probably the real reason was that they were too young and progressive and thus presented a threat to the leadership of the congregation.

It must be admitted also that there was considerable opposition to their views. Accusations of laziness were common and most damning among the Amish. Also the stance taken by these two couples was, in many ways, in conflict with the piety and theology of the quietistic and humble Amish emphasis.

Things were beginning to change in the Amish church, however, and after one or two furloughs both couples became the heroes of the more progressive element of the church. The example and influence of these two missionary couples, although difficult to measure, has been considerable among the Amish in Ontario. Quite a number of the writer's contemporaries can trace their own spiritual conversion to the dynamic preaching of Litwiller. In addition some of the young men who went to college and seminary and today are ministers and leaders in the Amish churches of Ontario, received much of their inspiration from the Litwillers and the Schwartzentrubers.

Both couples played leading roles in South America as well. Both men became bishops in the church there. Litwiller was also one of the founding fathers and first president of an inter-Mennonite seminary in Uruguay. While Litwiller became known more as a dynamic preacher and crusader, Schwartzentruber's strong points were his practical, commonsense administrative ability. Amos passed to his eternal reward in 1966. His wife lives with a married daughter in Argentina. The Litwillers, although officially retired and living in Goshen, Indiana, are busier than ever, both at home and abroad.

The two missionary couples mentioned above were responsible for the formation of a missions committee by the Amish conference in 1925. Challenged with the opportunity to support their own missionaries the conference appointed Christian Gascho of Wilmot, Menno Kipfer of East Zorra, and Peter Boshart of Poole to a missions committee whose main function was to collect funds for missionary support. A reorganization of the committee in 1938 left the organization with Moses O. Jantzi, Menno Kipfer and Daniel Wagler as members.

The 1940s were a time of spiritual awakening, bringing a new sense of mission. In 1943 the missions committee membership was increased from three to five members. Two years later the committee purchased a large old homestead in Tavistock with the intent to renovate it for a Senior Citizens' home. At the annual conference session in 1945 the missions committee was renamed the mission board and the following year conference purchased a vacated Presbyterian church in the town of Millbank for purposes of outreach.

Young People's Activities

The Anabaptist movement was a young people's movement to begin with. Its earliest leaders were comparatively young men, university students. Even the leader of the Amish division was referred to as a youth by his chief antagonist. The first Amish to come to Ontario were by and large young married couples, but alas, both Anabaptism and the Amish soon became old, not only literally, but also in spirit and attitude. As indicated in an earlier chapter, young people did not play a significant part in the life of the church. They were expected to join the church and attend but otherwise simply behave. Early activities included Sunday evening singings or parties with games and dancing.

Probably the man who did most to change this tradition was Jacob R. Bender, a minister in the East Zorra congregation from 1914-1947. Bender was largely responsible for starting a young people's Bible meeting in the East Zorra congregation in 1920. This type of meeting began in the 1890s following the John S. Coffman revivals, but really did not gain wide acceptance until after the 1920s. The East Zorra church was the first Amish congregation to adopt the innovation. Although aimed at older young people, they were largely young married people's meetings and some of the more progressive middle-aged people also attended.

Winter Bible schools attracted quite a few young people from 1930 to the mid fifties. These schools were concentrated studies of two to six weeks in length with daily sessions from 9:30 a.m. till 4:00 p.m. Monday through Friday. The teachers included a few local ministers and usually one or two visiting ministers from the United States. Most of these schools were held in the local churches, although the Wellesley Bible school was held for a number of years in Kennel's hall in the town of Wellesley. This was a six-week school with a six-year curriculum. The hall had kitchen facilities and served meals for students, some of whom had rooms in the village during the school term. A special feature of this school was an annual Christian Life conference which was usually very well attended. Through these years quite a number of young people from the conference attended Ontario Mennonite Bible School held at First Mennonite Church in Kitchener. This was an annual 12 week school with a three-year curriculum.

The next attempt at activity for young people among the Amish were the Literary Societies. These had their origin in general society in the 19th century and came into the Mennonite church early in the 20th century, just a little later than young people's Bible meetings. They were really the first organized young people's activity among the Amish. Again with the encouragement of the ministry, East Zorra was the first Amish congregation to organize such a society. It began in 1933, largely through the efforts of three young laymen, Walter Bender, Wilfred Schlegel, and Elroy Schwartzentruber as the Lend-a-Hand Literary Society. Other congregations also formed literaries although most of them quite a few years later. Meetings were usually held on a monthly basis and consisted of essays, talks, debates, and a newspaper, usually with considerable humor. The meetings were conducted in parliamentary style usually on topics of a non-religious nature. Their primary thrust was educational.

It must also be recognized that during this time traditional singings, parties, and dances continued among Amish young people. However, with more and more of the cultural barriers of language and dress removed more young people participated in non-Amish young people's activities. These included such things as community dances, movies, and sports. Althouah such activities were not sanctioned by the church they were nonetheless practised. Church-centered activities also began to bear fruit in a growing number of serious-minded and dedicated young people.

With the spiritual awakening, particularly among the young people, and their increased activities, a request was made to Conference to hold a youth conference. The request was honored and the first young people's conference took place in the Mapleview church on September 29-30, 1945. A young people's conference committee was formed, which for quite a number of years planned for an annual conference particularly for young people. This annual event played a significant role in providing inspiration and guidance for many young people during the forties and fifties.

11. First Sunday school conference at Steinman church at Baden in 1922.

12-13. Conference leaders Bishop Daniel Jutzi and Secretary Christian Brunk with his wife at time of golden wedding.

14-16. Other Amish leaders included Jacob R. Bender, Bishop and Mrs. Christian Schultz (center), and Bishop and Mrs. Samuel Schultz. The two bishops were the eldest and youngest sons of Menno Schultz.

More Change And More Involvement

7

A Sociological Overview

It is generally recognized that World War II was responsponsible for propelling Canada from a predominately agricultural economy into a more urban and industrialized one. The technological advances made during and following the war have continued to revolutionize life for most Canadians. The progressive majority of the Amish in Canada were no exception. They have quite readily adopted modern technology. When television made its appearance a few members felt the church ought to prohibit its use. However, the movement got little support from church leaders, many of whom remembered only too well the experience with radio referred to in an earlier chapter.

Amish farms, homes, and businesses have adopted all contemporary modern technology. Generally speaking, however, most have remained quite modest with a distinct emphasis on the family farm and business rather than on large commercial operations. The traditional Amish aversion to conspicuous consumption was not easily overcome. Technology did, nevertheless, lead the way in bringing about changes which transformed the Amish way of life for most.

Changes have also occurred in other areas although often with greater difficulty. The Amish emphasis on separation from the world, nonconformity to general society, and a strong sense of tradition have tended to lead to an equating of a particular cultural pattern with their religious tenets. Change became a threat to the faith of the fathers. Where such changes were necessary for survival, such as new methods of agriculture and the use of the English language in business, no great problem was evidenced. But to adopt new modes of transportation or communication, to become too involved in worldly affairs, or to change one's beliefs, patterns of worship, or other folkways was looked upon as sinful and wrong. For these reasons the rate of acculturation among the Amish was slower than among other people and in society in general.

The changes in technology accepted by the Amish simply confirm, as we indicated earlier, that changes in technology are always more readily accepted than are new ideas or religious beliefs. Another truth illustrated by the more progressive element of the Amish community is that once you begin to allow changes, it becomes ever more difficult to draw the line. Thus while acculturation has been a slow and a rather painful process in Amish society, it has been occurring and with increasing tempo in the last 50 years.

To illustrate we cite these examples. Fifty years ago the English language was not allowed in an Amish worship service. Today the only German used is perhaps an occasional hymn in some of the congregations. In 1920 all of the Amish were easily recognized by their distinctive clothing. Today, except for some older people, they dress like everyone else. In the twenties two Amishmen in the East Zorra congregation participated in local civic politics, were censured, and consequently left the church. Today a number of members have served, and are serving as councilors, reeves, and as mayor, while maintaining the blessings of the church. Where 30 years ago young people were censured for participating in sports such as baseball or hockey, today these activities are entirely acceptable. Many other similar illustrations could be given.

Acculturation has also occurred in more subtle ways. The acceptance of modern farm technology has tended to make the Amish about as independent as all other people. The welfare state has greatly undermined the traditional and practical aspect of brotherhood as formerly practised. Newspapers, radio, and television have influenced the religious thinking of most of the Amish to a far greater extent than most of them are aware. With the removal of most of the cultural barriers such as language, customs and religious sanctions, there is a general tendency to accept the value system of the surrounding contemporary society. On the other hand, there are serious attempts being made to keep a Christian perspective in the midst of this acculturation as we shall show later.

Urbanization

The Amish are still a predominantly rural people, although they are being affected by urbanization. While most of them live in rural villages or built-up areas, an increasing number of young people and older ones, too, are finding jobs in the city and making their homes there. Before 1950 there were no city churches. Presently (1972) there are two. An ever increasing number are engaged in other than agriculture or related activities. The early Amish who moved to town were invariably engaged in farm-related businesses. Noah Steinman, a member of the Wilmot congregation, opened a feed and seed store in Baden in 1904. Soon after this he apprenticed with a local mortician and became a funeral director as well as operator of a furniture store. In the same village Peter Gingerich purchased a cheese factory which has become famous for limburger and other cheeses.

In East Zorra Andrew Baechler purchased a farm implement business in 1910 and a little later also became agent for Ford motor cars. However, the activities of these early businessmen were held in question by their fellow churchmen and some of them ran into problems with the church. John R. Brenneman, also from East Zorra, for many years operated a typical country store in the village of Cassel. Both of the latter became involved in local civic affairs. Andrew Baechler was elected to the Tavistock town council in 1911. He became reeve in 1918 and served for five years. In 1927 he was again elected reeve and served in this capacity till 1934. Brenneman was elected to the East Zorra Township council in 1926 and served for a decade, the last two years as Reeve. Both men were censured by the church and consequently left the "fold".

In the Wilmot congregation, Samuel Steinman, farming adjacent to the town of New Hamburg and active in community affairs, was elected to town council in the 1930s but was not allowed to participate in the communion service of the church because of his political involvement. At the end of his term he decided to quit politics in order to stay in the good graces of the church. It was not until the fifties and sixties that the church's attitude changed enough to permit its members to serve in similar capacities without being censured. In the last ten years about half a dozen Amishmen have served as town councilors and reeves. Curtis Roth became the first mayor of the town of New Hamburg.

Since 1950 Amishmen have set up an increasing number of small businesses in local towns. In all but a few congregations farmers now are in the minority. Increasing numbers of younger people are living in surrounding cities or commuting to work there. An even more widespread "urbanization" has occurred by means of modern technology. In keeping with society in general, the gap between country hicks and city slicks has narrowed in our time also for the Amish. In addition to the automobile, which has provided easy access to the city, radio and television have brought urban sophistication into the homes of most people. Add to this the modern educational system with its consolidated schools, which most Amish children and young people attend today, and the end result is not appreciably different from an urban upbringing.

Most Amish homes today have all the modern conveniences and gadgets their city cousins have. Fewer young men are staying in agriculture. High land prices, expensive farm equipment, and a comparatively low return on investment, is making the risk involved foreboding to most young men. Whereas a generation ago most young Amish girls hired out as housemaids, today they work as secretaries, teachers, and nurses. Young men are finding jobs in town, going into professions, and a few into business and commerce.

For the first 130 years of their existence in Canada The Amish did not have a single church in the city. Perhaps the best symbols of the growing urbanization are the two city congregations they have today. One is in London and the other in Stratford, Ontario. In addition there are a number of Amish Mennonite churches in small towns. Many descendants of the Amish have left the denomination in the last 50 years, most of them now living in the cities of this country. A look into recent family histories and genealogies reveals that descendants of Amish pioneers live in almost every large city in North America.

Organizational Changes

Another area in which there has been considerable change among the Amish is that of organization. We trace these changes here primarily as they affected conference organization. In later chapters other changes will be delineated. Organizational changes came about partly through changing circumstances, the influence of the larger Mennonite brotherhood, and the presence in conference leadership of college and seminary-trained men.

The Sunday school conference remained basically a once-a-year mass meeting event until 1957. Previous to this, however, activities had increased considerably in the congregations throughout the conference. There was increasing cooperation with the Commission for Christian Education, a North American Mennonite inter-conference organization. This group suggested that area conferences organize to mesh with its own structure, which had assumed wider responsibilities with the increasing proliferation of activities within the church. Accordingly, a new organizational structure, the Christian Nurture Council, was adopted in September of 1957. The council consisted of an executive committee, plus a secretary for each of the following areas of activity: Sunday school, summer Bible school, winter Bible school, young people's Bible meeting, church music, home interests, junior activities, young people's activities and missionary education. The secretaries were the liaison between the churchwide Commission for Christian Education and the local congregations of the conference. The entire council was responsible to coordinate the total Christian nurture program in the conference.

Since 1957 there have been further changes, mostly to simplify the organization. A number of the activities referred to above have been combined and church camping has become an added area of concern for the organization. There has also been a closer cooperation with the Mennonite Conference of Ontario in these activities, although an attempt at organizational unity between the two comparable organizations failed to get approval several years ago. Changes in the overall church conference organization has put the chairman of the Christian Nurture Committee on the executive committee of church conference. Christian Nurture Council as such is no more. Instead, a committee of five persons seeks to assist and coordinate all conference activities. If necesary ad hoc committees are set up to take care of special needs. There are no more area secretaries. The committee works in cooperation with similar committees of two other Mennonite conferences in Ontario, namely the Mennonite Conference and the United Mennonite Conference.

The Sunday school was the first lay activity outside of the regular worship service. It was the first organized church-wide activity among the Amish in Ontario. Out of it grew a host of other activities included under the Christian Nurture Council which superceded the Sunday school conference. From the highly organized Christian Nurture Council has evolved the Christian Nurture Committee, which, although coordinating the same activities, is comparatively small and simple. From a once-a-year mass meeting approach the committee is following instead an area meeting design, usually emphasizing only one aspect of nurture in one such meeting. If any major event or thrust is planned, an ad hoc committee is usually appointed and then dissolved when the event is concluded. From one point of view these events may appear as having come full circle, having moved from simplicity in organization to complexity and back to simplicity again. These developments also show the church as being flexible, in tune with the times and circumstances, in order to accomplish the task of Christian nurture. Hopefully, the church will continue in this vein.

Two organizational changes took place in the mission board of the conference in the fifties. In 1950 the executive committee was enlarged from five to seven members, and three years later a decision made that each congregation elect a missions committee of three members. These committee members became members of the mission board by virtue of their office. This arrangement provided a closer tie with the congregations, and provided a contact for the board executive in each congregation.

Another purpose of congregational mission committees was to be alert to opportunities for witness and service in their immediate communities. A number of these committees organized missionary projects, fund raising activities, mostly taking the form of raising cash crops or livestock producing schemes in cooperation with farm members. It is not uncommon for some of these groups to raise several thousand dollars a year in this way.

With the increased mission-service activity of the board, and especially in light of the numerous properties acquired, the conference attorney, Maurice Andrew, suggested that the conference acquire a charter. This action was approved in late 1954 and incorporation became effective in January, 1956. The conference was chartered under the title, "Ontario Amish Mennonite Conference Inc." During this same time the Sunday school conference was reorganized and became the Christian Nurture Council as indicated above. With the many additional activities and organizational changes it was necessary to revise the church conference constitution as well.

The fifties also saw increased cooperation with the Mennonite Church and its church-wide conference organizations. Besides being a representative on the mission board, Henry Yantzi was appointed in 1956 as delegate to general council of General Conference and Ephraim Gingerich to its publication board. The Amish Mennonite Conference had also become a member of the Conference of Historic Peace Churches of Ontario. This organization was founded during the second world war to deal with government in matters related to conscientious objection to war. The writer represented the Amish in the Peace Problems Committee for a number of years.

The Conference also accepted an invitation in 1956 to appoint two men to the Rockway Mennonite High School board. This was a church-operated school in Kitchener, Ontario, sponsored by the Mennonite Conference of Ontario. In 1959 official action was taken, applying for full-fledged membership in Mennonite General Conference.

The 1960s brought more changes to the Ontario Amish Mennonite Conference. One of these was a change of name. It was decided to drop the term "Amish" because it was confusing to the general public, especially in outlying areas, and secondly, very few if any of the congregations in the conference were any longer practising the distinctively Amish practices of the founding fathers. In order to distinguish it from the Mennonite Conference of Ontario it was decided to designate the conference as the Western Ontario Mennonite Conference.

Inter-Mennonite cooperation also increased with participation in the Conrad Grebel College project. Since the late fifties a member of the conference had been involved in a study commission relative to the feasibility and desirability of establishing a Mennonite college on the campus of the emerging University of Waterloo. Following the study's positive report, all Mennonite and related groups were invited to appoint three persons to serve on the board of governors of the proposed college. The Ontario Amish Mennonite Conference responded by appointing Elmer Schwartzentruber, Dale Schumm, and Orland Gingerich in 1961.

In the same year, the conference agreed to a policy on cooperative church extension as worked out by the mission boards of the Amish and Mennonite conferences. Several years later this policy was revised to include the United Mennonites in Ontario, a third Mennonite body. These agreements resulted in several inter-Mennonite congregations. During the last decade the moderators of the three Mennonite groups referred to above have been meeting occasionally to plan cooperative ventures in other areas. Some of the committees of the three conferences have also been working together to avoid duplication and to pool resources.

In the middle sixties the Christian Nurture Council was further reorganized better to coordinate conference-wide activities. This move eliminated the winter Bible school board. Bible schools continued in a number of congregations but usually on a reduced scale. In the late sixties an organizational self-study was undertaken and further organizational restructuring accomplished. Where previously the organization had grown more complex, an attempt was now made to simplify conference machinery. In 1970 a new constitution and discipline was accepted, further illustrating this trend.

A rather significant organizational innovation occurred in 1966 with the adoption by the conference of a ministerial superintendent plan. Two years previously, the conference bishops had been asked to make a study of how best to deal with pastoral changes, ministers' tenure, retirement policies, financial support, and related matters. In 1965 the conference accepted in principle the suggestions put forward by the study committee, but requested further refinement and study of related areas. The plan, presented and accepted with a few minor changes the following year called for a ministerial superintendent who would serve as a pastor to the pastors of the conference and as a consultant to congregations relative to ministerial concerns.

About the same time conference authorized all ordained ministers to administer the ordinances of the church, a prerogative which had been limited to the bishops. However, since the number of congregations had tripled and only four active bishops remained, it was decided to allow all pastors to administer the ordinances rather than ordain more bishops. Another factor in adopting the plan was the increasing tendency for congregations to move in the direction of a trained and supported ministry in contrast to the traditional multiple lay ministry. A third major reason for change was a reaction against the life-time assignment of ministers in the same congregation. In 1970, along with the revision of the constitution, the designation ministerial superintendent was changed to conference minister to conform to other Mennonite conferences in North America who had also moved in this direction.

In contrast to the earlier conference organization, which allowed only ordained men as voting delegates (except for lay proxies), the 1964 session approved the appointment of lay delegates. Revision of conference constitution in the late sixties called for delegates from each congregation representing missions, Christian nurture, finance, and youth. Congregations with a membership of over 200 were allowed an additional delegate. In addition, all conference appointees serving on boards or committees were granted floor and voting privileges. This meant that lay delegates actually outnumbered ministerial delegates three to one. This represented drastic change from the middle fifties. At that time the lay delegate idea was rejected as posing too great a threat to ministerial authority.

The church conference has gone through the same process as the Sunday school organization, from simplicity, to complexity, to greater simplicity. At first it was purely a fellowship-sharing body. Then it became a source of authority. Later it met to conduct business. Now it is back to a more consultative, utilitarian organization. Currently all conference organization and activities are centered around the mission board, Christian nurture committee, finance and stewardship committee, and Mennonite youth fellowship. In order to coordinate all activities, the chairman of each of the above four organizations is automatically a member of the conference executive committee. According to the minutes of the inaugural meeting of this committee in 1971, its members saw themselves as fulfilling the following functions: coordinate existing program, serve as a sounding board, critically evaluate existing program, be creative, offer new ideas, give guidance, be congregation and people-oriented.

Mission-Service Involvement

Earlier in this chapter reference was made to ways in which the Amish became more involved in the life of their communities. That involvement was largely on an individual and personal basis. The mission-service involvement we are discussing in this section is a church-sponsored involvement in the mission of the church to share the gospel by word and deed.

Conviction to do mission work came to the Amish of Canada through the larger Mennonite brotherhood after the turn of the century. In its earlier stages it was related primarily to foreign missions. Only in the 1940s and later did conviction and action lead to an attempt to fulfill that mission at home. Bishop Moses H. Roth of the Mennonite Conference of Ontario is credited with helping to fan that spark to a flame during a winter Bible school session during the late 1940s.

The Mission Board operated a number of mission and service projects. The first venture in outreach was the purchasing of an unused church in Millbank in 1946. This mission existed for only a year, with Menno Zehr as superintendent, when the group decided to apply for congregational status. Quite a number of families who had been members at Mapleview and Poole chose to make their church home at Millbank. This made it possible for the group worshipping there to become an indigenous congregation in 1947.

About the same time there was a growing conviction among some families in the conference that another way of fulfilling the mission of the church would be to locate in some rural community and thus establish another mission outpost. The board assisted a number of families to rebuild neglected farm lands and to witness to the gospel. With the help of the Department of Agriculture one such location was found about 20 miles northwest of London, Ontario, near Ailsa Craig. Not only were there farms for sale, but also a church building which was purchased and renovated for the new congregation. In 1949 Wilfred Schlegel was ordained as minister.

Largely through the vision and drive of Schlegel, the congregation at Nairn used the proceeds of a missionary project of 100 acres of wheat to purchase a property in the city of London for the purpose of opening a rescue mission. The dream was realized in 1951 when Goodwill Rescue Mission opened its doors to minister to transient men and skid-row characters. Alvin N. Roth, one of the members who assisted in founding the Nairn congregation, became the director of the mission. In several years' time the quarters at the mission, despite the fact that transients were allowed to stay only four days a month, were no longer adequate for the demands made for its service.

After the mission became a member of United Community Services of the city of London in 1956, ensuing discussions led to the removal of restrictions as to the length of stay in order to alleviate the transient problem experienced in the city. This led naturally to serious overcrowding with no possibility of expanding facilities in that location. The next several years were spent in locating a suitable new site. A large downtown King Street property, offered at a very reasonable price, was chosen. However, due to opposition from merchants in the area and city zoning by-laws, this could not be utilized. Finally, a property was purchased on York Street and plans for a new building drawn up.

Several years earlier the church conference had approved a plan to appoint a local board of directors responsible to operate the mission. This board was composed of local church members and businessmen in sympathy with the work. The efforts of the board, together with help from officials of United Community Services, were of incalculable value in relocating the mission. Credit must also be given to city media for giving sympathetic coverage, to local churchmen and city officials for their moral and financial support. The city gave a grant of $26,000 toward the new building. This was matched by a $39,000 grant from the provincial government. Toronto Elevators, with whom negotiations had been carried on for the King Street property referred to above, sold their property for $10,000 more than they had asked from the Rescue Mission, then contributed that amount to the new mission building. Donations from congregations, friends, the conference, and a $7,000 gift from the Catholic church made up the remaining portion of the $150,000 building fund.

In the summer of 1961 the mission moved to its new quarters at 459 York Street. In the meantime the mission had grown in other ways as well. A country property was purchased near Wallacetown, about 30 miles west of London, in the middle fifties. The property, called 11th Step House had been used by an Anglican clergyman, Quinton Warner, as a rehabilitation center and was offered to the mission to be used for a similar purpose. In the middle sixties this property was sold and another purchased in London. It was named Quinton Warner House. A women's mission was also begun back in the fifties and grew till an additional property was purchased to house this work. In more recent years a teen girls' home has also become an integral part of the program.

When the mission moved from its original site at 536 Talbot Street it was renamed London Rescue Mission to avoid confusion with Goodwill Industries of London. Another change occurred with the move to a new site when the former advisory committee of local businessmen became the board of directors of the mission. With the ever-increasing activities of the mission and the complexity of the work, a completely new organizational structure was set up and adopted in 1970. The new organization, called Mission Services of London, is a completely independent and incorporated institution, although with a stipulated number of Mennonite representatives. The Western Ontario Mennonite Conference handed over several hundred thousand dollars worth of city property to the new organization.

Another branch of work gaining momentum under Mission Services is its family services program. Alvin N. Roth, superintendent of the mission from the beginning and now its executive director, was instrumental in instigating a maintenance and repair service to provide assistance to low-income, home-owning families wanting to make repairs to their dwellings. Presently the city of London and Roth are jointly working toward the establishment of a family center to be built on mission property. Also, since 1970 an experiment in ministry to low-income families has been carried on by the mission with Glen Horst as director.

In 1971 the London Chamber of Commerce honored Alvin Roth with its annual award for distinguished community service, thereby recognizing "his humanitarian involvement with, and great contribution to, so many citizens of London since the inception of Mission Services in 1951."

Also growing out of the rescue mission, at least in part, was the King Street Mission. A Sunday school and worship service were begun in a large dwelling in 1953. With the attendance of an increasing number of Mennonites in the city, plus community people, the congregation outgrew its quarters. A site for a new church building was chosen in the northeast section of the city in a new housing development. With the financial assistance of the mission board, as well as a $1,000 contribution from two other Mennonite mission boards, the congregation completed a new sanctuary in 1963. Perhaps the chief significance of the event was the fact that it represented the first inter-Mennonite congregation in Ontario. An agreement had been worked out with two other Mennonite conferences which made it possible to establish several other inter-Mennonite congregations in the following years, Valleyview in London being the first one.

A Sunday school and worship service were begun in the city of Stratford by the East Zorra churches in 1952. This move grew out of a summer Bible school held in the southeast section of the city for several years previously. There were also several resident Mennonite families in the city who were interested in forming a congregation. When the mission board assumed responsibility for the work, a house was purchased on the corner of Romeo and Brunswick Streets. With an increase in attendance the "church house" became too small and an additional lot was purchased on Brunswick Street and a new church building erected. This was dedicated on June 25, 1961. During the building process the group chose to call itself the Avon congregation. Avon, like Valleyview, was partially supported financially by the mission board, but within the last few years both congregations have become completely self supporting.

In 1963 negotiations began resulting in the establishment of a second inter-Mennonite congregation the following year at Parkhill, Ontario. A number of Mennonite families were living in the town and surrounding area. There was also a nursing and girls' home in Parkhill as well as a boys' ranch beyond the town, all staffed mostly by Mennonites under the leadership of Jack Wall. A large residence was purchased, renovated to include a chapel and Sunday school rooms, and dedicated in 1964 as Bethel Chapel. In the past several years the Mennonite population in the area has decreased, leaving further growth and development of the congregation in doubt.

Both Parkhill and Valleyview are under the administrative arm of the Western (Amish) Mennonite Conference with two other Mennonite conferences having contributed financially to their initial establishment. In turn, the Western Ontario Mennonite conference gave financial assistance to two congregations under the administration of the Mennonite Conference of Ontario. These two congregations are located at Listowel and Hanover, each having in its membership a number of families from the Western conference.

An area of service the mission board entered in the early fifties was that of rest homes. The Tavistock home, which had been purchased for this purpose in the middle forties but which could not be operated because of lack of support from the constituency, was brought into operation in

1953, and became known as The Maples Rest Home. With the financial backing and encouragement of some members of the Poole congregation a similar project was undertaken in the town of Milverton. The Milverton Home opened in 1955.

When, in 1967, new government regulations for such homes came into effect, the mission board decided it would be better to sell the two existing homes and erect a new one. In the ensuing discussion in conference a separate incorporated board, called Tri-County Homes was formed, with the express purpose of building and operating a new home for the aged. Three locations — in Tavistock, New Hamburg, and Milverton — were considered. New Hamburg was finally chosen. Several years elapsed before final government approval was granted and building operations begun. The building was completed in the spring of 1972 with a capacity of 96, including a three-bed sick-bay area. Nithview Home is located on the east bank of the Nith river overlooking the river and the town. Its unique architectural design gives each room a view across the river and over the town. The project cost over $1 million, part of which came from government grants.

The mission board also started a summer camp program for children from its city missions in the 1950s. For a number of years these camps were held on the bank of the Nith river in the Wellesley-Wilmot area. In 1962 development of a campsite in North Easthope Township, on the farm of Laverne Lichti, was begun and the campsite moved to that location. The site became known as Hidden Acres and was rented from Lichti for several years. Following discussions in mission board and conference it was agreed that the camping program should come under the direction of a semi-autonomous board of interested members. Accordingly a charter was secured, memberships sold, and the campsite purchased in 1964. Since that time there has been a slow but steady improvement of the site and facilities. In addition to children's camp, there are also young people's camps, a popular family camping weekend, plus many weekend retreats being held almost year round. Present plans call for further development.

Another significant service has been performed through the mission board from the early fifties when a student aid fund was set up to assist young people in acquiring post-secondary education. Because of its limited funds, seldom more than tuition was paid for any one student. However, dozens of students have been assisted over the last 20 years.

Students who received loans were expected to repay as they were able. Seminary students and others going into full-time church work were usually exempt from this requirement. Most of the people who are today serving in the foreign and home missions program of the conference, as well as a number of pastors and other church workers, teachers, nurses and social workers received assistance from this source. Most of those entering the "paying" professions have repaid their loans thus making the student aid program a revolving fund, continuing to enable young people to train for service.

A more recent approach to evangelism is that of placing bookracks in public and commercial places and keeping them stocked with good books. The past year saw more than 1,000 books a month sold through this approach. A number of other projects have been studied and undertaken by the mission board in the last year or two: a ministery to low-income families in the city of London, a work now assumed by mission services of London; a continuing study of the needs and possibilities for service to the transient tabacco workers in the Delhi area of southwestern Ontario; and a study and beginning program in regards to retardates and their families. A committee has been set up to work with representatives of London Psychiatric Hospital to find suitable homes for patients to learn to cope with life in a family context. The most recent project initiated by the board, with the main responsibility being assumed for its operation by a local group, is a youth hostel and drop-in center in the former Y.M.C.A. building in the city of Stratford.

Although there is nothing unusual about the activities recorded above they do indicate a revolution in outlook and approach of the Amish in Ontario. They also reveal a serious attempt not only to preach but also to practise the gospel, an idea that is in keeping with Amish theology and piety, although in an untraditional way.

Young People in Church Program

Some dramatic changes took place in activities among the young people beginning in the 1940s. One of the factors which triggered change was a spiritual awakening or revival. C. Z. Martin, a minister from Pennsylvania, was guest speaker at an annual Sunday school conference held at the St. Agatha church in 1942. In his concluding sermon he made a strong plea for Christians to dedicate their lives to God. An invitation resulted in numerous people making commitments. In the fall of the same year Martin was back in Ontario to conduct a series of meetings at the Steinman church. These services resulted in scores of young people and older ones making new commitments of faith. A young people's prayer-fellowship meeting which was started during the meetings continued for at least 20 years. Many other activities giving expression to the new spiritual life followed the experience at Steinmans. C. Z. Martin held other such meetings throughout the conference for a number of years following with similar results.

Some of the young people's activities were also due to new ideas and programs then in vogue throughout the Mennonite church. One of these was missionary projects. A common project in those years was raising turnips. These were sold and the proceeds donated to missions. Turnip hoeings and harvesting provided not only money for missions but enjoyable times of fellowship and a sense of involvement for young people. More active interest in the church and its services was very much in evidence. Greater participation by young people was evidenced in the Sunday evening young people's Bible meetings, in Sunday school teaching, summer Bible school work and in many other forms of expression and witness.

It was this new interest and activity among young people which was responsible for the young people's conferences which became very popular after 1945. In addition to the conference-wide meetings for young people, local congregations often sponsored weekend meetings dealing with such topics as choice of vocation, courtship, marriage, spiritual life, personal habits, and Christian ethics. During the fifties the Riverdale congregation at Millbank held annual missionary prayer conferences particularly geared to young people. Other activities included various forms of witness and service such as tract distribution and holding services in institutions and homes of shut-ins. With the voluntary service emphasis and program of the Mennonite church, many young people spent a year or more of time at home or abroad, serving in some charitable institution or mission program.

Another significant outcome of the spiritual awakening among the youth of the conference was that for the next 15 years a number of young people attended church colleges and seminaries. Previous to this, only two young people had taken any Bible training on the high school level and beyond. Verna Wagler and Alvin N. Roth were the first

Amish young people to attend Eastern Mennonite School in Harrisonburg, Virginia in the early forties. After 1945 there was a steady flow to Eastern Mennonite College, and to Goshen College and Seminary in Goshen, Indiana.

There were ten seminary graduates from the conference in the period between 1951-1961. Of the ten, three went into foreign mission work and the rest into pastorates, five in the Amish conference and two in the Mennonite Conference of Ontario. During this time the Amish had more seminary graduates than they could use. More recently that situation has changed. In addition to the seminary graduates there were other young people who attended the same school for shorter periods of time. At the same time more and more Amish young people were attending local high schools and teachers' colleges. While a trickle of young people still enrol at church high schools and colleges the majority attend state institutions. Thirty years ago young people who attended high school were an exception. Today the exceptions are those who do not attend.

Another change affecting Amish youth was the formation of a church-wide organization called Mennonite Youth Fellowship (MYF). The organization had its formal beginning in 1948 under the sponsorship of the Commission for Christian Education, an arm of Mennonite General Conference. An MYF manual was published to assist congregational leaders and young people to coordinate their activities and maintain a balanaced program. All young people's activities were organized around three main ideas: faith, fellowship, and service. In addition to the church-wide and congregational organization there is in Ontario a conference MYF. In the Western Ontario Conference the chairman of the conference MYF is a member of the executive committee by virtue of his office. On the congregational level the president of the youth organization also automatically becomes a member of church council. All of these factors indicate some of the tremendous changes that have taken place in relation to Amish young people in recent years, changes which are due to a large extent to changes in surrounding society but also a result of new spiritual life and vigor.

Issues of Church And State

8

Military Exemption

Christian Nafziger may indeed have had more than one reason to seek an audience with the King of England on his return trip to Europe. He was, undoubtedly, anxious to have his land deal confirmed by the Crown, but he was probably just as concerned about religious freedom. Oral tradition among the Amish in Canada insists that Governor Maitland had also promised Nafziger exemption from military service. However, years of experience in Europe had taught the Amish not to put final trust in lesser authorities. Many a nobleman who lured the Amish to his estate through promise of religious liberty was later overruled by the political rulers of the region. Furthermore, Nafziger's visit to the monarch of Great Britain also showed respect for proper authority and as such was well received.

That Governor Maitland gave assurance of exemption from military service is entirely plausible. Almost 30 years previously, in 1793, the Militia Act passed by the first Upper Canada parliament held at Niagara had granted exemption from militia duties, under certain conditions, to Quakers, Mennonites, and Tunkers. One of these conditions was the annual payment of fines by all male inhabitants from the age of

16 to 60. There is no record of any Amish paying these fines although being generally law-abiding they probably did. They had been accustomed to paying such fines in Europe prior to coming to Canada. Paying such fines was not a matter of conscience for them; it was simply giving to Caesar the things of Caesar as the scriptures plainly taught. The principle of fines as a substitute for militia service was not abrogated until 1849 after repeated attempts by representatives of peace churches to have them either modified or removed.

In any case, no serious conflict between the Amish and the state appears to have developed during the nineteenth century, although there was aversion to political involvement. This fact is further attested by the account of two Amishmen who were elected to local municipal councils early in the twentieth century. Both men were censured by the church for their involvement and consequently left their respective congregations. The Amish aversion to political involvement made such action unacceptable. This aversion was further strengthened by the happenings of World War I.

That the Amish considered the state more of an enemy than a friend is understandable in light of their experience in Europe. The gradual change in attitude evident by the turn of the century was probably the result of almost a century of peace and comparative religious freedom under Canadian government. World War I revived some of the antithesis between church and state so characteristic of Anabaptist theology and experience. A paragraph from a petition presented to the government during the war very aptly portrays both the Amish and Mennonite position:

> As a people we recognize the supremacy of the Lord Jesus Christ, whose kingdom 'is not of the world'. For this reason many of our people in all countries especially the leaders of congregations, have refrained from the use of their suffrage franchise, both for the sake of peace and harmony in the congregation and for the sake of a more complete separation from the entangling affairs of the world, although none are prohibited from the exercise of these privileges. Since the passing of the 'Wartime Elections Act,' we humbly seek to know the position of the government for all our members relative to this Act, so that we may conduct ourselves accordingly; realizing that in matters of war we cannot conscientiously give our voice, and in respect to government we are to be submissive to its laws, excepting only the higher laws of the Gospel in all righteousness.

It was the War-Time Elections Act which was particularly responsible for reinforcing Amish resistance to political involvement. Part of this act read: "All persons who shall have voted at a Dominion election held subsequent to the 7th of October, 1917, during the present war shall be held ineligible and incompetent . . . to apply for, or be granted . . . exemption." The Amish had, in cooperation with other peace churches, petitioned the government for exemption from military service for its young men when conscription was enforced in 1917. For the next 20 to 30 years the above government action was frequently used to discourage all political involvement including voting in any election. Despite this emphasis it was precisely during these years that Andrew Baechler, referred to above, was reeve and councilor in the town of Tavistock. Another older member of the Amish community in Wilmot Township has reported attending political meetings with his father during this time.

It is always dangerous to impute motives to other people but the feeling existed among the Amish that the law against voting by conscientious objectors was primarily a political move on the part of the Borden government to thwart the Amish and Mennonite vote which tended to favor the Liberals rather than the Conservatives. An even more negative interpretation from a present-day perspective would call such action political blackmail. A more positive interpretation on this action by the Canadian government might see it as attempting to protect the peace church groups and itself from the strong nationalistic and anti-German feelings which ran high in the country at that time. These feelings led to a change of name from Berlin to Kitchener and most young men were afraid to be seen in the downtown section of the city.

The actual exemption of young men from military service was handled through local tribunals. In order to gain exemption young men had to present certificates of church membership, duly signed by a minister or bishop of their respective congregation, indicating that the holder was a member in full fellowship before October, 1917. To the writer's knowledge no member of the Amish church was denied exemption, although this was not true of all groups in Ontario. Tolerance or the lack of it depended largely on the character of the local tribunal. A few young men, not very faithful members of the Amish church and not wanting to embarrass their ministers, left the country for the duration in order to avoid the draft. Religious conviction was, however, not the only basis for exemption. Any farm owner or farm laborer could get an exemption, providing his employer could produce evidence that he was needed to maintain agricultural production. All Amish young men applied for exemption on the basis of their religious convictions.

World War I had a sobering affect on the Amish church.

It halted a growing affinity with general society for it reminded the Amish that they were "not of this world" because of their pacifist position, and because they were German. However, such external pressure was not sufficient to halt the growing acculturation which had begun before the war. In other contexts we have tried to indicate some of the other side-effects of the war and so will not repeat these here. Suffice it to say the obvious: it was a maturing experience with both positive and negative results.

The second world war brought similar experiences with it. There was a repeat of the denial of voting privileges for conscientious objectors when Prime Minister King's Liberal government held a plebiscite asking for release from a previous election promise not to enforce conscription. The ensuing vote granted the government the right to conscript all able-bodied men, within certain age groups, into the Canadian army. There were, of course, exemptions for various reasons. One of these included conscientious objection to war.

In the meantime representatives from various Mennonite and other peace churches had organized a Conference of Historic Peace Churches. A military problems committee, which had been formed by several groups previous to this, now became the negotiating committee between the peace churches and the government. It handled all matters related to conscientious objection to war and in turn interpreted government policy to its member churches. Later this committee was also charged with the responsibility of providing for the spiritual welfare of the young men serving in alternative work camps.

Through negotiations between the Conference of Historic Peace Churches and the government a policy of alternate work camps for conscientious objectors was worked out. Young men were to serve for four months in camps operated by the Department of Mines and Resources. Later the men were required to serve for the duration of the war, and the work camps were brought under civilian control through the Ministry of Labour. Work performed by the conscientious objectors included road building, forest protection, national parks, and agriculture. In addition to their maintenance, the young men received 50 cents a day. From 1943 on men were placed individually on farms and factories to aid in maintaining the country's production. Men on farms were paid $25 a month plus their maintenance. Factory workers received $38 a month without maintenance. In all cases, however, the employer paid a full wage with the remainder of the wages going to the

Canadian Red Cross. Conscientious objectors across Canada contributed well over $2 million to the Red Cross during World War II.

During the first world war very few Amish young men enlisted in the army. While no accurate figures are available, a small percentage voluntarily joined Canada's armed forces during World War II. Possibly the main reason for this was the growing acculturation which had taken place prior to 1940. One of the side-effects of the war was the growing involvement of Amish young people in the voluntary service program of the Mennonite church. The post-war period was especially fruitful in this respect, although the ongoing service program of the church has not lacked volunteers in more recent years.

Another post-war development involving the Amish to a limited extent was the civil defence movement in the 1950s. This again became an issue in which the military problems committee of the Conference of Historic Peace Churches involved itself. After negotiations with government officials it was agreed to have representatives from the various constituencies of the Mennonite brotherhood take some training at the Civil Defense College in Arnprior, Ontario, and then return to inform their own people. About the same time a new organization, called Mennonite Disaster Service, was being formed in the Mennonite churches all across North America. The organization was founded to aid victims of natural disasters such as floods, tornadoes, storms, or earthquakes, by cleanup and reconstruction work.

In discussions with civil defence officials it was mutually agreed that, should a national disaster in any form come to Canada, members of the peace churches could serve through their own MDS organization. While willing to work under civil defense, the peace churches made it clear that they did not want to become involved in military operations. Their position was clearly stated as follows: "We will willingly render every help which conscience permits, sacrificially and without thought of personal safety, so long as we thereby help to preserve and restore life and not to destroy it." Although the emphasis on civil defense has abated, the Amish, with the Mennonites, have continued to serve through MDS, not only in times of disaster but also in cities across North America in assisting low-income families with improved housing.

The Welfare State

The Amish have at times also come into conflict with the

state relative to some aspects of its welfare program. Their emphasis on separation of church and state, plus a very practical concept of brotherhood, have caused them to reject all offers of government aid. A statement on government aid was drawn up in 1945 in a meeting of the ministerial body of the Amish Mennonite Conference of Ontario and later circulated to all churches in the conference. With the preface pointing to "Christian principles and home relationships and obligations, as has been maintained and upheld by our church since coming to this country over a century and a quarter ago . . .," the statement urged members to refrain from receiving government aid such as family allowance, mothers' allowance, and old age pension.

Despite this brave attempt to forestall involvement in the welfare program of the government, members of the conference churches have increasingly accepted such benefits. In fact some of the very men who helped draw up the statement referred to later accepted old age pension cheques. Reasons for this quiet acquiescence are no doubt many; the growing adjustment to society, government aid to farmers in the form of subsidies, a less restricted view of separation of church and state are certainly some. As indicated earlier, the Western Ontario Conference has for some years been accepting government aid, grants, and loans in its service programs in various communities.

It is only fair to say, however, that there are still many members who do not accept such government aid. The Old Order Amish in Canada do not accept any such aid even today. Although the conference as such no longer prohibits its members from participating in the government's welfare program, and even itself actively seeks government grants, it does so only when it is assured that receiving such aid will not restrict it from operating in accord with its principles. Probably the greatest current threat of the welfare program is the fact that it threatens to rob the church of expressing its traditional brotherhood concept in a practical way. What long-range effects this will have remains to be seen.

As indicated above the Old Order Amish still do not accept any government welfare aid. The most vexing problem for them the last few years has been the compulsory Canada Pension Plan. To the Amish this is a form of life insurance and as such is contrary to their principles. However, through the persistent efforts of Mennonite Central Committee and Elven Shantz, a retired Mennonite businessman, this situation is changing. The federal government is currently in the process of revising its statutes to provide exemption for the Amish from participating in the pension plan. The fact that the Amish do not accept other government hand-outs, or welfare payments, and do take care of their own members' needs, was no doubt a major factor in the government's decision to exempt them from the Canada Pension Plan.

Another aspect of the Amish protest against the welfare state is what we might term their work ethic. They believe it is wrong to get something not worked for. They also tend to look at the welfare system as undermining personal responsibility and encouraging laziness and graft. In the simple rural life-style of the Amish, older people do not need a pension. They live with their children, although usually in a separate part of the house. They usually have some income from the farm which they owned and the children are now paying for. Family allowance is looked upon as a government device to claim the lives of the children, especially sons, in the event of war. Since none of these government aids are compulsory they pose no problem. The Amish simply do not apply for them.

Education

While the Amish in the United States have been fighting a running battle with the states over the matter of education the situation in Canada was quite different until very recently. Reference was made to an earlier chapter that in almost every area the Amish settled they served on the initial community school boards. Throughout the last 150 years members of the church have served on section school boards. The Amish are very much for elementary education. Their emphasis on personal responsibility does not only apply to work and material things. Salvation and church membership are a matter of personal responsibility so that the ability to read for oneself is most essential in religious matters as well.

It is true, however, that the Amish have always shied away from higher education and this meant anything beyond the eighth grade. This explains their conflict with American authorities where school attendance is compulsory to age 16 rather than 14. This is not the only reason, but perhaps the most dominant one, for the current Amish objection to state education. The Amish naturally object to the "new-fangled" ideas and emphases in education. They object to their children, and especially the girls, wearing gym clothes such as shorts. They object to the commonly held and taught concept of evolution which to their understanding is contrary to biblical teaching. In Canada it is only in the last few years, since consolidated schools have become standard, that the school system has created problems for the Amish.

Despite the traditional exclusiveness of the Amish, they have never tried to isolate themselves from others in their communities. As far as the writer is aware the idea of separate schools was never given any consideration in Canada before consolidated schools made their appearance. Even now not nearly all the Amish send their children to separate schools. Many still patronize public schools. In most cases teachers and principals of public schools respect parents' requests, and exceptions are made for Amish children in relation to objectionable features of the school's program. It is only where no such consideration is given that the Amish resort to establishing their own schools.

Although there might appear to be a tremendous "culture gap" between the Amish way of life and modern culture, there appears to be no major obstacle. Children are told simply that the Amish do not live like other people because this is what the Bible teaches. This explanation plus good relations in the home and with other people in the community, despite the differences, is usually sufficient to see the child through grade school without causing any serious problems for either parents or children. The Amish attitude of "live and let live", unless that attitude is not reciprocated takes care of the differences.

Aversion to higher education is subtly instilled by the use of satire and humor. Jokes and stories depicting the stupidity of the so-called educated person are common among the Amish. Despite this attitude the writer remembers one of the highlights of his adolescent years as being a one-day visit to the Ontario Agricultural College in Guelph, during the annual farmers' week. In the area of religion the inference is invariably made that the inspiration and guidance of the Spirit of God is irreconcilable with education and especially seminary training. This bias to theological training is probably a reaction against the Anabaptist experience following the Reformation, when the educated religious leaders of the state churches were the most vehement enemies of the forefathers. In more recent times part of its motivation may have stemmed from an attempt to defend the Amish practice of an uneducated lay ministry.

In the previous chapter reference was made to the changes in both attitude and practice of the members of the more progressive element of the Amish community in relation to education. Although some of the old attitudes linger, members of the Western Ontario (Amish) Mennonite conference as a whole cooperate with the state system of education including the secondary and university levels. This does not mean they are uncritical of the present educational program. It does mean they are working within it and probably will not make any attempt at separate schools. Whether or not the conservative or Old Order groups will continue to move in the direction of separate schools will depend largely on how insistent the state school system will become in enforcing its own regulations. One member of the brotherhood has stated that if the government educational authorities had not been so unbending in their demands there would be no separate Amish schools in Ontario today.

In concluding this chapter it needs to be said again that the Amish are not anti-state. They are, in fact, very respectful of and obedient to the state. It is only when the state demands of them something which their religious conviction forbids that they refuse to comply. While they will petition for privileges they never fight for them. Hence an Amishman would never go to court to protect himself. A good case in point is the welfare and education issues. Although the Amish in Canada have gained exemption from participation in the Canada Pension Plan, it was won largely for them by others. The same is true of the school attendance issue in the United States where the Supreme Court handed down a decision favoring the Amish. In that case likewise it was not the Amish, but friends of the Amish, who took the battle to the courts and won.

Both of the above victories need to be seen in the larger context of religious freedom. Despite the exclusiveness of the Old Order Amish, and their stance of non-involvement in politics, they have become a catalyst in procuring a freedom which gives hope that not all distinctive societies in North American will be forced into a common mould. In their nonconformity the Amish may have made a major political contribution to modern society.

17-18. Montreal River Camp 43 scenes show Amish Mennonite COs: Orland Gingerich (author), Edgar Kennel, Walter Steinman, Orville Jantzi, and Erwin Bender. Visiting Mennonite leaders are Peter Nafziger, first non-bishop moderator of conference, J. Harold Sherk, and J. B. Martin.

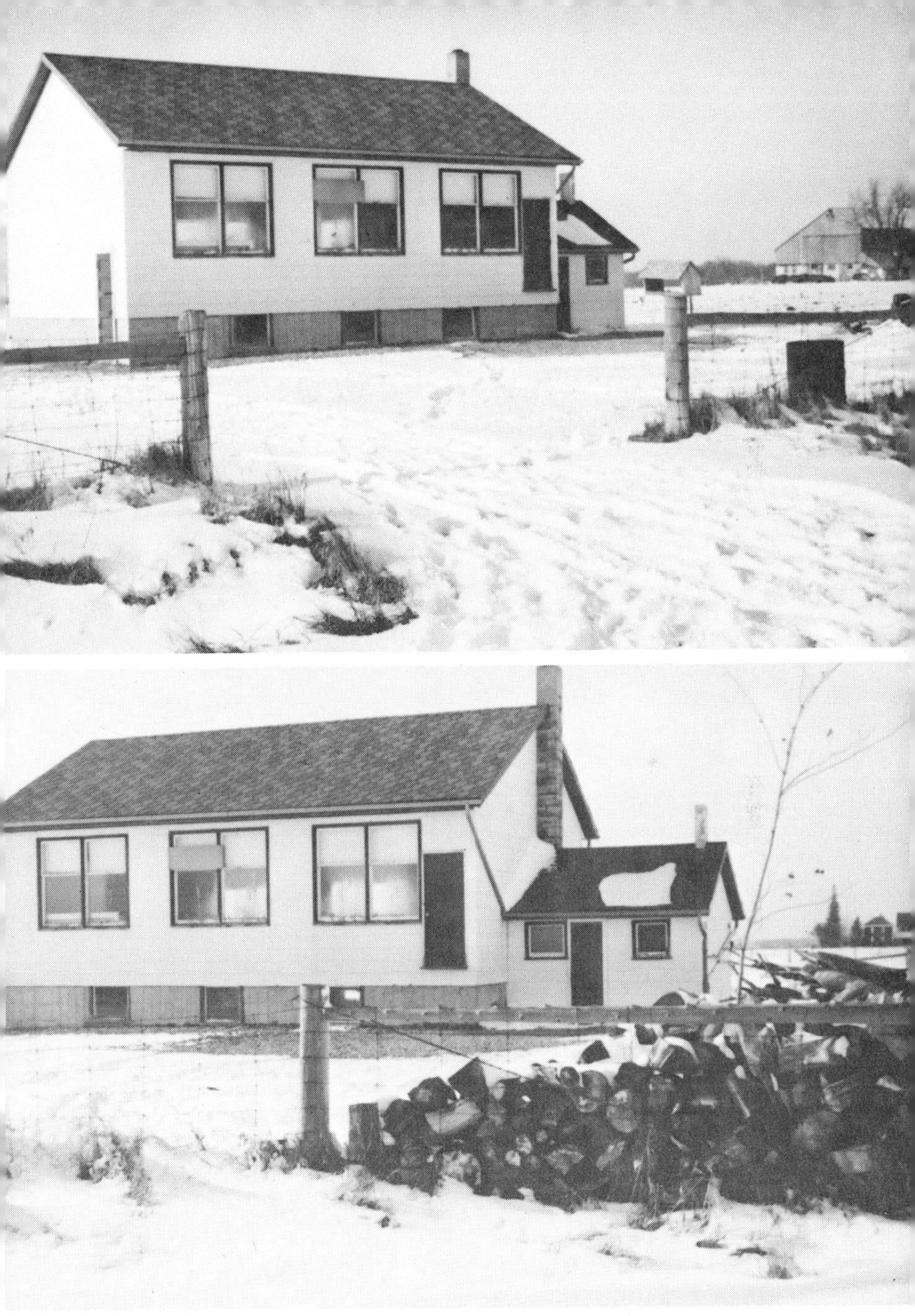

19-20. Education. In the 1960s the Old Order Amish established their private elementary schools.

Congregational Expansion And Development

9

Wilmot

The reader will recall that when meeting houses were built in the 1880s the Wilmot congregation erected two buildings, one in the northeasterly section of the township just west of St. Agatha on Erb Street, and the other referred to as the Steinman church west of Baden on Snider's Road. Services were conducted alternately with both ministers and Sunday school superintendents serving at each place. The reason for the two places of worship probably relates to the fact that previously services had been held alternately in the two general localities because of the size of the congregation as well as its geographic spread.

It was not until 1939 that decision was made to hold services at both places every Sunday. Ministers and Sunday school superintendents continued to alternate, however, for the two were still considered one congregation. As time progressed the people attending at either place became more separated. selection of trustee boards for each church property was the first step in forming independent congregations.

In 1946 the group decided to erect a new building at Steinman's. For years the old building had been inadequate, especially for Sunday school, since it had no basement. The original building was torn down and work begun on a new structure. The project was completed in spring, 1948, resulting in a brick structure with the main sanctuary, including a balcony, seating 600 people. The basement provided much needed Sunday school rooms, a small auditorium, kitchen facilities, etc. In addition, the original lot was landscaped providing ample parking and additional space for playgrounds which were used during summer Bible school and later for a kindergarten and nursery school.

There was no similar need for additional space at the St. Agatha meeting house. Over the years as families moved off their farms they tended either to gravitate to Baden, New Hamburg, or Waterloo and Kitchener, resulting in a decreasing attendance. In 1948 it was decided to rearrange at least the inside of the building. The pulpit was placed on the west side facing lengthwise rather than broadside as it had been originally. The pews were rearranged accordingly, the wooden stoves removed, and a furnace installed. A few years later a basement was added. The old building was jacked up, given a quarter turn, and placed on the new foundation with a new front entrance added. The new basement and remodelled church were completed in 1953, providing much better facilities for the increasing activities of the congregation. It still took another five years, however, before the two congregations became separate entities.

St. Agatha

It was not until 1957 that the St. Agatha congregation became a completely independent congregation but the process had been going on for some time. Peter Nafziger, who lived near the church, became pastor of the congregation. In 1960 a younger man, Gerald Schwartzentruber, was ordained as minister. Allen Schwartzentruber was ordained as deacon. Membership figures have not changed very much in this period, with about 130 persons currently comprising the adult membership.

In 1968 the congregation received a bequest toward the purchase of an organ from a former life-long member of the church. Following some congregational meetings concerning the use of musical instruments in the church it was agreed to acquire an organ for a trial period. Traditionally, the Amish have been against the use of musical instruments, especially in connection with worship. However, following the trial period the congregation voted in favor of making the organ a permanent installation. The church became the first rural congregation in the conference to use an organ in its worship service. The only other congregation in the conference using one before this was Valleyview in London, Ontario. Since 1956 a young couple from the church, the Victor Dorsch family, has served as missionaries in Africa, with the congregation supplying their financial support.

Steinman's

Most of the membership of the Wilmot congregation gravitated toward the Steinman church. This was natural in a sense since this meeting house was geographically more central to the Amish population in the township. In 1957, when Steinman's became a separate entity, the membership was around 400. Again the membership has not changed very much since that time. In fact the membership of the Wilmot congregation as a whole has grown very little in the last 50 years. In other ways this church, like most in the conference, has changed considerably during the same period. We will be discussing some of these changes in a later chapter.

Elmer Schwartzentruber became the first stationed minister in the congregation with the writer serving as the bishop of both Steinman and St. Agatha congregations. In 1961 Emmanuel Steinman was ordained deacon. Following Orland Gingerich's resignation as active pastor of the congregation a younger man, Albert Zehr, served at Steinman's till 1971. The congregation has experienced some difficulties in the last several years. Tensions due to the tremendous changes, both in leadership and in ideological and theological positions, plus the generation gap, have all tended to make the necessary adjustments difficult. Mixed with this are the seemingly inevitable personality clashes in such situations and the stage is set for a traumatic period of development.

In other ways the congregation has been a leader in adopting many of the newer trends so evident in the Western Ontario Conference churches in the last 20 or 30 years. Early in the 1960s the Kenneth Schwartzentrubers were commissioned to serve as missionaries in Brazil. Both originally from Steinman church the couple had served in the Nairn congregation before going to South America. In the last 20 years five additional young men from the congregation have trained for the ministry and are, or have, served in various churches in Ontario. Numerous other young people have served in short-term projects of the Mennonite church both at home and abroad.

East Zorra

This has been the fastest growing church in the conference since the 1920s. In 1925 the original meeting house on the 16th Line was enlarged in order to accommodate the growing congregation. Ten years later the enlarged building was again overcrowded. Consequently a vacant church building was used and later purchased. This church was located on the 17th Line of East Zorra Township, several miles southeasterly from the original church. In less than ten years the 16th Line church was once again too small. By this time an increasing number of Amish lived in the town of Tavistock and the near vicinity. Accordingly, services were begun in the town's library hall in 1942. Several months later a Presbyterian church was rented and services held there till 1949 when the building was sold. Rather than purchase the older church building the congregation decided to build a new one, completed in 1950. Despite these two additional places of worship the 16th Line church was still crowded, particularly for Sunday school, since the old church had no basement under the main building. Early in 1951 the congregation decided to remove the old building and erect an entirely new structure. Later the same year the new church was dedicated, complete with basement, classrooms, kitchen facilities, a Sunday school assembly room, and a main sanctuary upstairs seating over 500 people.

By the early sixties this new building was once again overtaxed. This time expansion resulted in construction of another new church just west of New Hamburg. A survey of the membership taken by the congregation revealed a concentration of members in that area with a considerable number living in town. A new church building was erected and a congregation organized in 1964. The congregation is known as Hillcrest and is located in Wilmot Township. Since 1940 the original East Zorra congregation has expanded to four places of worship, although prior to 1950 the ministers alternated among the three churches. In that year the ministers were stationed but the three churches continued to operate as one congregation until 1964 when the Hillcrest church was organized.

There probably were a number of reasons for the greater growth and development of the East Zorra congregation. The congregation was more rural than the one in Wilmot. A more pertinent factor may have been a more charismatic leadership. Jacob M. Bender, to whom reference was made earlier, was the only bishop ordained without the use of the lot by the Amish in Ontario. He served immediately before and after the turn of the century. From the twenties to the forties the congregation again had two rather outstanding leaders: Jacob R. Bender, a more scholarly and progressive man was minister, and Daniel Jutzi was bishop. He also was a very devout man and progressive in many ways, but his greatest contribution was his preaching and emotional appeal.

The greater openness of the leadership in East Zorra during this time made it possible for other outstanding men to minister to the congregation through special meetings, Bible schools and conferences. One can only speculate what other reasons there may have been for the tremendous growth of the congregation. The fact remains that total adult membership before the separation into four congregations reached over 900, almost double that of the Wilmot congregation.

Following the organization of four independent congregations in East Zorra the original meeting house continued to be known as the East Zorra church. Stationed in this congregation as ministers were Daniel Wagler and Andrew Zehr, the deacon. Several years after the ordination of a younger man, Dale Schumm, some differences arose both in the leadership and in the congregation. Consequently, it was decided that both Wagler and Schumm should discontinue their services and a new minister, Newton Gingrich be asked to serve. While Schumm went to India as a missionary Wagler became the leader of a group which left the congregation to set up an independent congregation. Further particulars of this group will be given in a later chapter. The present membership of the East Zorra congregation is about 300.

Following the death of Deacon Andrew Zehr the congregation decided in 1969 to appoint two elders to assist the pastor in his work. The two men appointed were Howard Bender and Nelson Yantzi. Pastor Newton Gingrich was from the Mennonite Conference of Ontario and was at that time (1966) actually the moderator of that Conference, a position he held while serving as pastor of a congregation in the Western Ontario Conference. This incident merely points up the new attitudes which exist between the Mennonites of Amish origin and other Mennonites in Ontario.

As indicated in previous chapters, this congregation was the pioneer in the twenties and thirties by first adopting young people's Bible meetings, winter Bible school, literaries, as well as being the first congregation to erect a meeting house in the previous century. More recently the young people of the four East Zorra churches have been active in drama, producing a number of plays. The congregation has also partially supported several foreign missionaries and taken an active part in home missions.

Cassel

The Cassel church got its name from the small hamlet of Cassel located nearby, and was, as indicated earlier, the first extension of the original East Zorra congregation. Until 1950 the congregation was served by ministers from the mother church. From 1950 on Joel Schwartzentruber served as minister and Daniel Zehr as deacon. The present pastor, Vernon Zehr, is assisted by two appointed elders, Howard Gerber and Glenn Zehr.

Although the church has not grown much numerically, it has developed into a very vital congregation. The past several years have seen a slight decrease in numbers, due largely to people leaving the rural area for town and city. If this trend continues the Mennonites may find themselves in the same situation as the Evangelical church did 40 years ago when it sold the present church building to the Amish. A member of the church, Mary Jane Brenneman, served several terms as teacher in a mission school in India. The congregation provided for her financial support. In the last several years the congregation has had some interesting ecumenical exchanges with neighboring United and Lutheran churches. In the writer's opinion the congregation will play a vital role in the foreseeable future.

Tavistock

Begun in 1942 Tavistock congregation has had a slow but steady growth. This probably reflects two trends; that of retiring farmers moving to town instead of building an addition to the farm home, as the custom used to be, and the increasing number of young people working and living in town. Some members of this congregation also live in Stratford but still have their church home in Tavistock. The current membership of the congregation is about 225.

The first permanently stationed minister in the congregation was David Schwartzentruber. From about 1958 to 1964 Henry Yantzi, bishop of the East Zorra congregations assisted Schwartzentruber in the ministry at Tavistock on a part-time basis. Peter Erb, a young man from the congregation and a graduate of Waterloo Lutheran University, assisted in the ministry for one year as a licensed minister (1966-67). When he left to complete theological studies in Toronto the congregation appointed two elders, Millis Leis and Ivan Bender, who became responsible to administer the church program. The Tavistock congregation was the first church in the conference to appoint elders in this presbyterian sense. The current pastor is Wilmer Martin, originally from Pennsylvania, who has served the congregation since 1968.

The first minister of the congregation, David Schwartzentruber, served as a relief worker under Mennonite Central Committee in Poland for a period of time following World War II. In 1960 his son Earl was ordained and commissioned to serve as a missionary in South America. The congregation provides part of the financial support of the Schwartzentrubers in Argentina. Richard Benders, a young couple from the congregation, have just recently returned from a two-year service assignment in Haiti. A number of members of the congregation are deeply involved in the town's civic and community affairs. In 1969 the congregation remodelled the church building, adding a spacious new front entry.

Hillcrest

This last extension of the East Zorra church continues to function under the leadership of Henry Yantzi, formerly bishop of the East Zorra churches. Yantzi was also moderator of the conference for many years, and contributed vitally to the development within the conference churches during the past 20 years. Vernon Brubacher, a local high school teacher, and Mahlon Bender, a semi-retired farmer, assist the pastor as appointed elders. Membership figures have not changed much since the beginning although there has been a slight increase. The present adult membership is just below 200.

The congregation is actively interested in the wider outreach of the church. It provides financial support for two adult missionaries, one in Israel and another in South America, in addition to several missionary children. It also has a very active young people's group involved with the other East Zorra churches in music and drama. A number of young people from the congregation have served in the voluntary service program in a number of different areas. With the trend from rural to urban living the congregation has good prospects for numerical growth, situated as it is close to the growing town of New Hamburg.

Blake

In 1920 the Blake congregation, located in Hay and Stanley Townships of Huron County, was numerically the smallest in the conference. For many years leadership was provided by a local deacon with assistance from other ministers in the conference. In 1940 Deacon Solomon Baechler was ordained as minister. In 1947 a younger man, Ephraim Gingerich, was ordained to assist. Gingerich was ordained bishop in 1952 becoming the first resident bishop since the death in 1850 of the founder of the congregation, Bishop John Oesch. Gingerich served till 1971. Since 1966 he has also been pastor of the Zurich Mennonite church, which had originated after a division in the Blake church in 1908. Negotiations to unite the two congregations have been under way for several years.

A small rural congregation, the church has also been affected by the growing urbanization; membership has been decreasing rather than increasing. There has been active cooperation with the Zurich congregation for quite some time and both could benefit from a merger. Cyril Gingerich, former missionary to Africa, served as interim pastor till June, 1972, when Clayton Kuepfer assumed pastoral responsibility of both congregations.

Mapleview

Growth in this congregation led to a decision to build a new meeting house in 1928. Like the other early buildings the original structure had no basement. The new structure was of frame with a full basement and continues to serve the congregation. With an increasing membership the building became inadequate by the middle forties. When several families left to help form the Millbank congregation the congregation was slightly relieved. Several years later an unused Presbyterian church in Crosshill was purchased and a second congregation established. In typical Amish fashion the two churches were administered as one congregation. In 1967 ministers were permanently stationed at each church, although it was not until 1970 that they became separate congregations.

The Mapleview congregation has tended to be more conservative than other conference churches. Part of the reason is its close proximity to the Lichti congregation and the fact that quite a few members of this more conservative group have transferred their membership to Mapleview.

For quite some time the congregation has had a very active group of young people who have served both in the congregation and beyond. Alvin N. Roth who heads Mission Services of London, is a former member of the congregation. The administrator of the new Nithview Home for the Aged in New Hamburg was also a member of this church. A number of others have served in mission-service assignments. Current membership is around 300 persons, with Alvin Leis serving as minister and Jacob Roes as deacon.

Crosshill

Begun in 1949, as indicated above, the attendance was never very large here until after 1970 when it became an independent congregation. Organization as a separate church was actually the result of a more conservative stance, not shared by all the members, taken by the bishop of the Mapleview congregation. Consequently, those members who were not in full agreement were given the opportunity to transfer their membership to Crosshill. The current membership at Crosshill is approximately 160. Steve Gerber is minister and Ervin Erb deacon of the congregation.

The congregation in spring of 1972 completed extensive renovations and an addition to their church building, providing facilities for Sunday school classes and other activities. Since the church as a separate entity is still very young, it is difficult to characterize it. However, it shows promise of becoming a vital congregation within the Western Ontario (Amish) Mennonite Conference. The old part of the present church building has an interesting history. Former members of the Presbyterian church have presented a plaque to Crosshill in commemoration of its early pioneer founder and builder.

Mornington: Poole

This, the youngest of the five original Amish congregations in Canada, has had some difficult periods in its history. In the aftermath of two divisions in less than 20 years bishop oversight was assumed by a sister conference in the United States. In 1926 the congregation once again had its own bishop in the person of Christian Schultz. Despite its difficulties the congregation grew making for crowded conditions in the old meeting house. A basement under the meeting house gave additional space for Sunday school classes. The organizing of a congregation in nearby Millbank in 1946 relieved the situation as some families transferred to that church.

A leadership crisis occurred again in the 1940s following the inability of its older bishop, Christian Schultz, to continue serving. Moses H. Roth, a Mennonite bishop from the Ontario Conference, was asked to serve and did so until 1959. In the meantime, Herbert Schultz, a young man of 19, was chosen and ordained in 1955 to assist in the ministry. After completing a four-year Bible course at Eastern Mennonite College Schultz returned to assume pastoral responsibilities. The years that followed were times of growth and maturing for the church. In 1965 the congregation completed building a new and modern church building which serves the present membership of 300.

Following the resignation of Herbert Schultz to complete his theological training, the congregation called Amsey Martin as full-time pastor of the church. Martin is assisted by two elders, Nick Schmidt and Alvin Schultz. The congregation has had a very active program with many of its young people becoming involved in a number of the church's mission-service projects.

Millbank

Adopting the name Riverdale this congregation had its beginning in 1947, only one year after its beginning as a "mission". The membership, as was suggested earlier, was composed mainly of families from the Wellesley and Poole churches. Soon, however, a number of Old Order Amish families who had experienced a spiritual renewal also joined the Riverdale fellowship. The congregation has a current membership of nearly 200.

Menno Zehr, appointed superintendent of the "mission" in 1946, was ordained as the first minister of the church in 1948. A year later Valentine Nafziger was ordained as deacon. When it was decided in 1951 to ordain a bishop for the congregation the lot fell to Nafziger. When a few years later some differences arose because of a more conservative stand by Bishop Nafziger, the conference attempted to mediate in the dispute. Nafziger and a number of families felt they could not accept the proposed conference solution and left the church to form an independent congregation. Menno Zehr has continued as pastor in the Riverdale church, assisted since 1958 by David Jantzi, also ordained a minister at that time.

Despite the disruptive influence of the division, Riverdale

has had a growing and maturing experience. Additional families of Mennonite background have relocated on farms in the area and are making it their church home. There has been a very active youth program in the church. For quite a number of years young people of the congregation have sponsored a missionary-prayer conference. Others have served in the voluntary service program of the church. One young man from the congregation, Clayton Kuepfer, has just recently been installed as pastor of the Blake-Zurich churches.

Nairn

Brief reference was made in an earlier chapter regarding the beginning of the Nairn church in 1948. The congregation has never become very large, partly because a sizeable portion of its membership is composed of people working in several institutions in the community. The group is, therefore quite mobile. Current adult membership is a little below 100.

What Nairn lacks in numbers it has made up in spawning a number of mission and service projects. In addition to the London Rescue Mission mentioned earlier, a rest home was opened in Ailsa Craig, a boys' farm for delinquents was begun and then turned over to Mennonite Central Committee. Later the congregation operated a mission farm in an attempt to give young couples a start in farming. The most recent service project is "Friendly Acres," sort of a halfway farm home for patients from London Psychiatric Hospital. It is an attempt to help such people once again cope with life outside of a hospital.

The pastor of the congregation, Wilfred Schlegel, has been a dynamo behind all these projects. He has been assisted during the years by a number of young men of various Mennonite backgrounds. This roster of young men graphically reflects the varied background of the congregation. Kenneth Schwartzentruber (Amish) served first until he and his wife accepted a call as missionaries to Brazil. Daniel Zehr (also Amish) served for several years until he accepted an assignment as executive secretary of MCC (Ontario). He is currently serving as executive secretary of MCC (Canada) in Winnipeg, Manitoba. Myron Schrag (GC) assisted for a two-year period and Melvin Otterbein (United Missionary) also served for two years. John Brubacher (Mennonite) served for a year and a half. Currently the congregation is experimenting with a "team ministry," composed of Schlegel, Nelson Scheifele, and Jim Helmuth.

Avon

The Avon congregation in Stratford began as a Sunday school which developed from a summer Bible school conducted in the southeast section of the city for a number of years. Floyd Baechler was the early superintendent of the mission. From the middle fifties till 1962 Jacob Spenler served as pastor of the church. Kenneth Bender then became pastor serving till 1966. Serving as interim pastor for two years was Arthur Leis, a missionary on furlough from Africa. Winston Martin, a young man from the Mennonite Conference of Ontario and a graduate of Toronto Bible College, assumed the leadership of the congregation in 1968. He was ordained as a minister by the conference in 1970 and continues to serve as pastor of the Avon congregation. The membership of the congregation is about 25 although average attendance is considerably higher.

Valleyview

For the first ten years worship services in the city of London were held in a large, old dwelling on King Street. The congregation had its beginning in 1953 with Alvin N. Roth, superintendent of the Goodwill Rescue Mission, serving as pastor. With increased duties at the mission, Roth could not continue as pastor. In 1961 the congregation extended a call to Ralph Lebold who came to London following his graduation from Goshen Seminary. Having outgrown its quarters on King Street the congregation decided to build a new church. A site was chosen in the northeast section of the city in a comparatively new housing development. The new church building was dedicated in June of 1963. Located on an elevation, it overlooks an extensive valley to the west towards the University of Western Ontario, hence the name Valleyview. Lebold has continued as pastor of the congregation although he spent portions of the past several years attending Crozier Seminary in graduate study as a counselor. During this time others in the congregation and ministers from the area filled in for Lebold. Walter Friesen, a Mennonite Brethren student in the city and a member of the congregation, was licensed by the conference to serve as interim pastor for a year.

More recently the London congregation is making a unique contribution by serving as an in-service-training center for seminary students from Associated Mennonite Seminaries in Elkhart, Indiana. For a number of years three students from the seminary have come to Valleyview each year for their time of practical training. Student response to the experience has been enthusiastic. The students assume most of the pastoral duties with Ralph Lebold serving as supervisor. Lebold spends most of his time as assistant chaplain at London Psychiatric Hospital. Also working in and from the congregation is a former student intern, Glen Horst. The rest of Horst's time is given to a ministry to the low-income families of the city, a project sponsored by an inter-Mennonite organization. The current adult membership of the congregation is about 85.

Zion

The Zion congregation, located in the town of Wellesley, was begun in 1953 by Elkannah Kennel in an attempt to reach the unchurched of the town. The first number of years services were held in Kennel's hall, also used for winter Bible school. Later, services were moved to a small United Church in town and shared with that congregation. Solomon Bast was appointed as lay preacher and continues to serve the congregation. The adult membership is about 25.

Bethel Chapel

This congregation in Parkhill, Ontario, about ten miles west of Ailsa Craig, is an inter-Mennonite group which came into being in 1964. Membership was originally composed of a number of families who lived and worked in the town and several members from Nairn who lived in the vicinity. In addition Mennonite employees of a girls' home and another boys' home in the area attended here. A large, older dwelling in Parkhill was purchased and remodelled as the congregation's place of worship. It was named Bethel Chapel. John Brubacher was licensed in 1964 to serve as pastor of the congregation. In 1966 Brubacher was ordained and continued to serve until 1969 when the congregation accepted his resignation. Leonard Epp, a minister of the Conference of Mennonites in Canada, became pastor in 1970. Actually, membership was never very high and always quite mobile. In the last year a number of families have moved out of the area leaving the future of the congregation in jeopardy.

Summary

When the Ontario Amish Mennonite Conference was formed

in 1923 there were five congregations with a total membership of less than 1,500. Almost 50 years later there are 16 congregations with a membership of about 2,800. In addition, some members have become part of other inter-Mennonite congregations not under the administration of the Western Ontario (Amish) Conference. Such congregations are located in Listowel and Hanover. On the other hand, inter-Mennonite congregations under the administration of the conference have also brought in some members of non-Amish background. These congregations are Valleyview in London and Bethel Chapel in Parkhill.

The growth indicated above is by no means phenomenal. Many of the descendants of the Amish have left the church of their fathers and become members elsewhere, or completely neglected the church. A few have become near famous, like Beland Honderich, publisher of the Toronto Star, whose great-grandfather was one of the early Amish pioneers in Wilmot Township, where Beland grew up as a boy. On the other hand, at least some branches of families such as the Schultzes, Brunks, Waglers and others have become members of the Amish mostly through intermarriage.

In the last 100 years the Amish of Ontario have spread to other parts of Canada (although there were never any distinct Amish congregations outside of Ontario) as well as to most of the United States. Through the mission, relief, and service programs of the Mennonite church they have served on every continent except Australia. In Ontario they have also spread over a much larger area in the past 20 years. The direction has been largely into the southern and northwestern counties of the province. The one exception is an Old Order Amish congregation located in eastern Ontario near Belleville. Will the Amish continue as a distinct group or will the present trend of acculturation and assimilation cause them to disappear from the Canadian scene. We will attempt to speak to that question in the following chapters.

21. The first Amish meeting-house was built at Zurich in 1885 and will remain in use until the planned merger of the congregation with the Zurich Mennonite Church takes place.

22-23. Older and newer styles are reflected in these two Beachy Amish meeting-houses of the Nafziger and Lichti congregations built around 1904 and 1963, respectively.

24-25. The East Zorra and Tavistock churches, in rural and urban Tavistock, respectively, were both built in the 1950s.

26-27. Variations in church style appear also in these contrasting photos of the Mapleview and Steinman churches built respectively in the 1920s and 1940s.

28-29. Among the Presbyterian church buildings purchased by the Amish Mennonites and adapted for use in the 1940s are those at Millbank and Crosshill.

30-31. More contemporary church styles were adopted by Hillcrest and Poole churches in the mid-1960s.

Immigration From The U.S.A.

10

Reasons for Coming to Canada

So far our story of the Amish of Canada has centered on the original immigrants who came from Europe in the 19th century. We turn now to look at a new and more recent wave of Amish immigration to Canada. This part of the story is not altogether unconnected with the former. An Amish community in Southern Ohio was forced to move because of the American government's plans for the area. Secondly, some of the new immigrants were direct descendants of a former Canadian Amish family.

In contrast to the Canadian Amish, who settled in only one province and in closely adjacent communities, the Amish in the United States scattered into more than 20 states. One obvious reason for the difference is the much larger Amish population in the United States. Other possible reasons may be the prohibitive cost of land in the older Amish communities, forcing them to look elsewhere for settlement possibilities, and the traditional Amish attempt to get away from the "world," especially in areas where they came into conflict with government over school attendance and other issues. Until very recently the Amish in Canada did not have any of these conflicts with the government.

In 1952 the Atomic Energy Commission of the United States chose the hill country of Pike County in southern Ohio as the site for a large atomic plant. Six Amish families who had moved into the area only a few years earlier now were forced to find a new location. A few additional families from Daviess County, Indiana, and one from Jerome, Michigan were also interested in moving to a new location. After discussing possible sites a tour was conducted through Kentucky and Missouri but no location decided on.

In the fall of 1952, a number of boys busy filling corn silos were talking about their favorite sport — squirrel hunting. One of the older boys brought a map of Canada one day and told of the wonderful hunting and fishing area in the Georgian Bay area of Ontario. This fired the young men's imagination. How about moving to Canada to settle? The boys' fathers were not as enthused about that prospect as their sons. They likely shared a common American concept of Canada as a land of cold and snow. In fact several of the Pike County Amish families were direct descendants of John S. Wagler, a deacon in the East Zorra congregation in Ontario, who had moved to Indiana in 1871. Wagler apparently had not appreciated the cold Canadian winters and so had moved south.

Despite these unfavorable first reactions to the idea of settling in Canada the families decided at least to investigate the possibilities. The investigators returned with enthusiasm to migrate. The country had no military conscription; even though young Amishmen in the United States were exempt from military duty they did have to participate in an alternative service program. This took the boys away from home and into potentially unwholesome environment.

Canada looked like a good place to settle for several other reasons. There were no rigid school attendance requirements beyond elementary education. They could even have their own schools if they desired. There were no compulsory farm programs or social security, all of which had gotten the Amish into trouble with United States authorities. In addition, the Canadian border officials in Windsor assured the Amish they would be welcomed as immigrants.

Pleased with these findings, the Amish proceeded to Chatham and enquired about available farms. However, land prices around Chatham were too high so they continued to London. Alex Enz, a real estate salesman in that city knew of some farms for sale in the Aylmer area where he had once lived. Aylmer is about 20 miles southeast of London, in an area of good farm land. Well satisfied with the farms, the men returned to Ohio to make plans to emigrate.

New Settlements

In December of 1952 four Amish families purchased farms near Aylmer, Ontario. They were Peter Yoder and Homer Graber of Daviess County, Indiana; Simon Leroy Marner of Jerome, Michigan and David Wagler of Piketon, Ohio. The Yoder and Graber families arrived in Alymer on March 5, 1953 to take possession of their farms. Other familes soon followed, including two from the original Ontario settlement in Milverton. By the middle sixties more than 20 Amish families were living in the Aylmer area. Most of the farms are located north and east of the town of Aylmer.

There have been numerous changes in the Aylmer settlement since 1965. A total of 18 families have moved out of the community. Six of these returned to Pennsylvania, six went to Missouri, and another six to Honduras in Central America. Despite this drain there are still 16 families left in the area. Jacob Eicher is the only ordained man who has not moved away. He serves as deacon of the congregation. Elmer Stoll and Simon Wagler are the ministers. There is no resident bishop at the moment.

The Aylmer settlement was the first of ten in the next 15 years. As one writer put it, "Canada fever" ran high among the Amish in the United States. The fever has also subsided for many of them as the records reveal many families have returned to the United States or moved elsewhere. Two settlements have become extinct — a small colony near Wallacetown, 30 miles southwest of London, and one near Lucknow north of Goderich, where the last families moved away in spring of 1972. Part of the reason for the failure of the Wallacetown settlement was a change in Canadian immigration policy in the sixties. For a time there was some feeling against the Amish taking over Canadian farms. This has changed, however, and recently quite a number of Amish have again immigrated.

The second colony established by American Amish was located in Sullivan Township, Grey County. It is commonly referred to as the Chesley District, located in the Chesley-Williamsford area about ten to 20 miles from Owen Sound and Georgian Bay. The first families to arrive came from Tennessee, shipping their belongings and livestock by train.

Joseph Stoll graphically relates their introduction to the canadian winter in the following account.

> In December of 1954, these first Amish at Chesley made trip after trip to Williamsford with their teams and steel-tired wagons, bringing to their new homes the contents of the boxcars that had arrived from Tennessee. A few days before Christmas, the temperature suddenly plunged below zero, and the stiffly-frozen snow screamed in protest as the steel wheels of the wagons rolled homeward. It was too cold to ride, and the teamsters walked alongside their wagons, heads down as they faced the wind, clapping their thick-mittened hands together as the cold crept through to the fingertips.

A second wave of immigrants arrived in Chesley in 1961-62. These people came from Ohio and increased the population to the size where the community was divided into two districts or congregations. Since these Old Order Amish still worship in homes there is a very definite limit to the size of a congregation. A number of families in this settlement have again returned to the United States. However, the total population has not decreased due to natural population increase. The Chesley group represents the "Schwartzentruber people," one of the strictest Amish groups.

Another settlement founded about the same time was the one near Norwich in Oxford County only about 20 miles northeast of the Aylmer colony. Most of the families in this area came from Holmes-Wayne County, Ohio, with a few also from Conewango Valley in New York state. One of the larger settlements, this one was also divided into two congregations in 1963. A number of families from here started a new colony in Eastern Ontario several years ago. Otherwise this community has not lost very many members.

Leadership in the west district of Oxford County is composed of Abe Troyer, bishop; Dan Stutzman Jr., minister; and John Stutzman, deacon. East district bishop is Eli Schwartzentruber with Levi A. Miller and Daniel E. Gingerich serving as ministers. Atlee Shetler is the deacon. The Amish have their own schools in this area, as they do in several other communities. In most of the larger settlements they also have machine, or carriage shops, where they produce their own carriages and also serve people in surrounding communities.

A second settlement in Oxford County, usually referred to as Lakeside, is located about five miles southeast of St. Marys. Four families took up residence in this area in 1959 coming from three different states. The following spring two of the families moved to a new settlement about 12 miles east leaving the future of the settlement very much in doubt. In the summer of 1960 a John Mast family from Delaware came to join Deacon Elmer N. Yoder who had also come from Delaware. The following year things began to look up as five families from Stark County, Ohio moved to Lakeside. This group included Bishop Noah Coblentz.

For the next several years additional families arrived from a number of different states. By 1966 there were 22 families with an adult church membership of nearly 60 and a total population of 134. However, in the following years a number of families, eight in total, again left the settlement, some going back to the United States and others to a new Canadian settlement. This colony has the distinction of drawing its members from the greatest number of American settlements. The 20-plus families at Lakeside came from ten different areas in the United States. Currently 14 families reside in the community.

As indicated above two families from the Lakeside settlement, Jacob and Henry Hertzlers, moved to Tavistock area in 1960. These were followed by another Hertzler family the same year and about five more from Pennsylvania and Maryland. The settlement never grew very large. It is, in fact, the smallest colony of Amish in Ontario today, numbering only four families at present. Most of the families moved back to the United States with one emigrating to South America.

Also begun in 1960 was a colony near Gorrie in Huron County about 30 miles northeast of one of the original Amish settlements begun before 1850. Most of the settlers in this community came from Dover, Delaware. While a number of families from this settlement have moved elsewhere the colony has enjoyed a steady growth. From 11 families in 1966 the community has grown to 20 today. The Amish do not have their own school as yet but are considering the possibility. Noah S. Byler was recently ordained bishop of the congregation to assist the senior bishop Simon S. Byler. Ministers are Levi Hersberger and Dan Byler. The congregation does not presently have a deacon.

Two separate communities of Amish were begun in 1962, the one near Wallacetown referred to earlier and which became extinct in 1964, and the second one at Mt. Elgin. The latter is located about ten miles north of the Aylmer settlement and approximately the same distance east of Norwich. Although experiencing some of the same problems as the Wallacetown group due to a tougher Canadian immigration policy, this community has survived.

Most of the original settlers in the Mt. Elgin area came from Iowa. Later a number of families from other areas also moved in. By 1966 there were only seven families in the settlement. Beginning late the same year additional families began arriving after the relaxing of immigration policies. In 1972 there were 26 families, making it one of the larger of the new Canadian Amish colonies. Spiritual leaders of the congregation include Enos Yoder, bishop; Ministers John Kauffman and Ed. Petersheim and Deacon Joni Miller.

In the fall of 1967 a number of young men from the Norwich settlement went deer-hunting about 100 miles northeast of Toronto, Ontario, in the Belleville-Stirling area. The hunters lived in a vacated farm house during their expedition and found a number of deserted farms. The discovery fired their imagination. Why not return and buy these farms and form a new settlement? The response back at Norwich was positive resulting in several families moving to the area later the same fall. By 1972 there were nine families in the settlement. They include five Shetlers, three Masts, and one Miller family. Enos J. Miller and Rudy N. Shetler are ministers with Levi Mast serving as deacon.

The latest settlement occurred in 1969 when five families, all from other Canadian settlements, moved into the Lucknow area. This community is located about 20 miles west of the Gorrie colony in Huron County. Since that time two families have moved to Paraguay, and a third returned to Pennsylvania. The two remaining families expected to move out before the end of 1972. It appeared this settlement was also doomed to extinction.

This concludes our survey of recently established settlements in Ontario. A few years ago some Amish investigated the possibility of immigrating to Eastern Canada; however, no action resulted, leaving Ontario as the only province with Old Order Amish settlers. While immigration has slackened off considerably there are still a trickle of families coming from across the border. What the future holds no one can tell. The fact that most of Canada's welfare payments are on a voluntary basis and that in the future the Amish are to be excempt from the compulsory Canada Pension Plan may well increase the flow again.

As was indicated earlier, for a period in the sixties there was opposition to the Amish taking over Canadian farms. This feeling, not shared by all Canadians, seems to have subsided. In most cases the Amish have settled in rural areas where younger people were no longer taking an interest in farming so that they can hardly be accused of taking farms away from Canadians. In most areas where they settled, the Amish have improved the agricultural economy of the community. While they are not big operators, or prolific spenders, they are, generally speaking, good farmers and appreciated by their neighbors.

The New Canadian Amish

A very obvious difference between the original Canadian Old Order Amish and the new immigrants is in their vehicles of transportation. Most of the Americans have entirely enclosed carriages, including windshields, whereas the original Canadians use only completely open buggies. Among the Old Order Amish in the Milverton area even top buggies are taboo. There are, of course, other minor differences in both groups, although basically their concepts and outlook are quite similar.

Another distinctive feature of the new Canadian Amish, particularly the Aylmer group, is their aggressive publishing venture. Prior to 1964 there were only two distinctively Amish periodicals. One of these was The Budget, published in Ohio since 1890. Begun by the Amish the paper was taken over by the Royal Printing Company, an outside organization, in 1920. The paper continues, however, to carry much Old Order news and is widely read by them. The second paper is "Herald der Wahrheit" (Herald of Truth), an Amish periodical first published in 1912 by the Mennonite Publishing House at Scottdale, Pa. Taken over by the Amish Mennonite Publishing Association of Kalona, Iowa, in 1956, the latter has become the official church periodical of the Old Order Amish both in Canada and the United States.

In late 1963 three men from the Aylmer settlement, David Wagler, Jacob Eicher, and Joseph Stoll, together with Levi J. Lambright of La Grange, Indiana, formed the Pathway Publishing Corporation. The organization received its charter early in 1964. Its objectives were to publish and distribute select Christian literature to Amish and other homes. Basic printing equipment, including an 11 x 15 offset press, a folder, a paper cutter, and a stitcher was purchased. The machinery was set up in a temporary shop on the Jacob Eicher farm and powered by a diesel engine. In the summer of 1966 a new building was erected, also on the Eicher farm, where the publishing venture is now located.

In addition to a number of periodicals, Pathway Publishers has numerous booklets as well as larger cloth covered works to its credit. The latter have been printed for the firm by a commercial printer. Pathway does not as yet have binding facilities. Besides printing equipment and storage and office space, the new building has a small retail outlet for its pamphlets and books.

Perhaps nothing has flourished like the periodicals published by Pathway. The first one, The Blackboard Bulletin, is a 24-page monthly published in the interests of Amish schools and homes. It was first begun as a private venture by an Amish teacher, Joseph Stoll, who became its editor when it was taken over by Pathway. In January of 1966 a second paper made its appearance under the title, The Ambassador of Peace. This magazine is especially geared to Amish young men in alternate service in the United States, but has actually expanded into a more general youth magazine, with an ever growing circulation. The editor is Calvin E. Anderson, a young Amishman from Orrville, Ohio. Family Life, the title of a third Pathway magazine, is "dedicated to the promotion of Christian living with a special emphasis on the appreciation of our heritage." This periodical has also found wide acceptance among the Old Order and other conservative Mennonite and Amish groups.

From the writer's viewpoint the greatest contribution the new Canadian Amish are making to their spiritual brothers in Canada is through the literature they are producing. Only the future will tell the effects this influence is having on the original Old Order Amish of Canada. There has been some personal interaction between the two groups. A few of the original Amish families have taken up residence in the new colonies and there has also been some intermarriage. Some of the new groups have participated in the Amish Mennonite Fire and Storm Aid Union of the Canadian Amish.

Although interaction between the new Canadian and Canadian Amish has been limited, hopefully it will continue to grow to the mutual benefit of each. One of the limiting factors in this respect is the jealously guarded congregational church government and the traditional aversion to anything new or different. While these factors may not change much in the near future we believe there is genuine spiritual life among the Old Order brethren, and that this will continue to transform what is merely traditional.

The Unchanging Old Order

11

Resisting Trends and Fashions

Quite in contrast to the fleeting fashions and styles of dress and grooming of modern society are the typical 18th century European styles still worn by the Old Order Amish without very much change. Like their Old Order Mennonite counterparts, the Amish have effectively resisted change. In fact Amish patterns of dress go back further than do the Mennonite styles. This is true largely because the Amish tended to put more emphasis on dress and grooming than did the Mennonites. An Old Order Amishman can easily be distinguished from his Mennonite brother by his beard and longer hair. The Old Order Mennonite is always clean-shaven and fastens his clothes with buttons while the Amishman still uses hooks and eyes.

A few years ago a newspaper cartoonist depicted a hippie approaching an Amish couple on a street corner with the question, "Hey man, where did you get that groovy outfit?" Styles have obviously come full circle. Some of the emphases in the current youth culture, turned sour as it is on western civilization's materialistic value system, are quite similar to the simple life style of the Amish. Current interest in the Old Order groups, however, is not limited to youth. There appears to be widespread popular interest in distinctive groups who have not allowed themselves to be pressed into the moulds of contemporary trends and fashions.

Coupled with this popular interest is the Canadian government's current emphasis on multiculturalism. The mood fostered by the emphasis on appreciation for Canada's varied cultural heritage, will hopefully lead to greater tolerance and respect for distinct cultural and minority groups like the Amish. Such attitudes and circumstances provide an excellent opportunity for the Amish to witness to the larger society. However, the Amish are more concerned with preserving their heritage than they are in propagating it. Their exclusiveness prevents them from aggressively sharing their beliefs and practices with others. To open the door to the outside world would be a real threat to the things they hold dear. Any person serious about learning from them would be welcome, but outsiders merely inquisitive about their lifestyle are soon under suspicion of attempting to exploit them. Despite this popular interest it is not likely because of their religious orientation and rather severe discipline that very many people will join the Amish. Nevertheless, their unchanging ways, unhurried pace, and emphasis on primary relationships hold a certain fascination for modern man.

The reader will recall that the Old Order Amish originated in 1886 when the majority of the members in the Wellesley and Mornington Amish congregations decided to build meeting houses in which to worship. Prior to 1883 all the Amish worshipped in homes. Although no division occurred in East Zorra, Wilmot or Hay Township congregations over the meeting house issue, not all the members in these congregations were necessarily in favor. In fact, after the division in Wellesley and Mornington, quite a number of families from the former congregations joined the Old Order group, which functioned as one congregation till 1891.

Since all of the bishops were in favor of meeting houses and so stayed with the larger group, the Wellesley-Mornington Old Order congregation did not have a resident bishop until 1891. In that year bishops from the Old Order church in Holmes County, Ohio, who had served the congregation up to that time, ordained Christian L. Kuepfer as bishop of the Mornington congregation. At the same time Peter Jantzi was ordained as minister in the Wellesley group to serve with Deacon Joseph G. Jantzi, who had been part of the group from the beginning. From this time on the Wellesley-Mornington groups became two separate congregations. Bishop Christian

L. Kuepfer from Mornington served as bishop of both congregations until 1902 when Peter Jantzi was ordained bishop of the Wellesley Old Order congregation. The two congregations held worship services on alternate Sundays, making possible a continuing fraternalization.

Agriculture and Business

Until 1945 there were only two congregations of Old Order Amish in Canada and they were the two referred to above. There continued a slow but steady growth of the two, primarily in a westerly direction further into Perth County. In relation to Amish tradition and practice the two congregations changed very little during this time. With a few exceptions, such as carriage shop operators and carpenters the Old Order Amish are farmers. The Amish have their own construction business, although for the most part the people are also farmers. Young Amish girls usually work as maids, primarily among their own people but someties also for outsiders.

The most outstanding exception to the above generalization was the Ebersol self-feeder manufacturing establishment in the town of Milverton. John Ebersol, a young Amishman from Pennyslvania, courted and married a young Canadian Amish girl from the Wellesley Old Order congregation. Ebersol did custom threshing for his brethren in his home state. They returned after their marriage to the United States where John had begun experimenting with a self-feeder for threshing machines. Previous to this threshing machines had to be hand-fed. Sheaves were thrown on to a stand in front of the cylinder of the threshing machine and a man was required to cut the bands and feed the grain into the cylinder, a dangerous and unpleasant job to say the least.

Returning to Wellesley Township in 1908, young Ebersol that summer assembled his first self-feeder in his brother-in-law's machine shop. Later the same year he moved to the outskirts of the town of Milverton in Mornington Township where he set up a shop and began producing self-feeders for threshing machines. The Ebersol self-feeder soon became a by-word and was shipped all over Canada and the United States.

Despite Ebersol's successful business venture he remained a typical, simple Amishman all his life. An incident repeated frequently related to a travelling salesman's visit to the Ebersol plant. Like a typical Amishman Ebersol wore a straw hat most of the time, even in winter, in his plant and office.

Inquisitiveness got the better of this particular salesman and he asked Ebersol, "Why do you wear a straw hat all the time?" "To keep my head cool so I can mind my own business," was the quick reply. The incident aptly illustrates the wit and humor so characteristic of the Amish.

The Steckley District

In 1945 there was a division in the Old Order congregations in Ontario. While this was perhaps partly due to the growing Mornington congregation which made worship in homes difficult, there were also growing differences and personality conflicts within the congregation. Consequently, a new congregation was formed with Samuel Steckley ordained as minister and Menno J. Kuepfer as deacon. A year later Steckley became bishop of the new congregation. He served till 1969 when William Carter was ordained bishop. Two additional ministers have also been ordained, namely Aaron J. Kuepfer in 1953 and Kenneth Kuepfer in 1968.

The Steckley district, as it is usually referred to, is more progressive and open than the other Old Order congregations. Since 1966 members of this group have permitted the use of such modern technology as the telephone, electricity, tractors and other modern farming equipment, as well as automobiles. They have also adopted newer ideas and practices in church life. In addition to the regular bi-weekly service, they conduct a Bible study and a choir practice on alternate weeks. The choir practice is in reality a singing school rather than practice for a performing group. They do not sing separately in a regular worship service.

In most other ways the congregation follows very much the traditional Amish forms of worship and other practices. In 1972 the membership of the congregation amounted to about 30 families, nearly 100 adult members. Counting children and young people not yet members, the total attendance is near capacity for a house church. Geographically this congregation is on the northwestern edge of the Amish community in Mornington and Elma Townships.

Other Old Order Congregations

Due to growth in numbers, basically by natural population increase, the original congregation in Wellesley Township became too large to worship in one home so the community was divided into two districts or congregations. People living north of the 7th Line formed the northeast district, while those on the south became the southeast district. Members of both of these congregations spill over into Mornington Township although the majority live in Wellesley.

About ten years later, in 1970, the original Mornington congregation, too, again became too large and was divided into the upper and lower west districts. In actuality the upper district is more strictly a central district since the Steckley district is located on the northern edge of the Amish community. In summary, this means that the two original Old Order congregations in Ontario have grown to five in number since 1945 when the Steckley group was formed. In a sense the Steckley congregation fits better into the Beachy Amish pattern, and was so listed in an Amish church calendar in 1971. However, the group considers itself Old Order.

Another interesting phenomenon is happening in both Wellesley and Mornington Townships. Over the years as the non-Mennonite population tended to move off the farms the more progressive Amish took over these farms. Currently as these people are leaving the farms and becoming more urbanized the Old Order people are moving into the area slowly being vacated by their more acculturated brethren.

Four of the congregations named — upper and lower west districts and north and south east districts — have accepted a minimum number of changes. They do not permit their members to own any modern machinery except stationary gasoline engines for threshing or chopping grain, pumping water, or running milking machines. Milking machines have only been accepted very recently. Even though the members of the four Old Order congregations are not permitted to own tractors they do get custom-operated tractors and machinery to do some of their farm work. The same is true of modern means of transportation; although not allowed to own cars they are permitted to ride in them or get neighbors or friends to take them on longer trips.

Membership figures of the Old Order congregations are difficult to obtain since the Amish tend to shy away from keeping records. The biblical basis for this aversion is the story of King David's numbering of the children of Israel in the Old Testament, an act for which he was severely punished. Furthermore, such numbering of their people might become an occasion for pride in growth of numbers. Records of the Fire and Storm Aid Union indicate over 150 "policies" taken out by the Old Order Amish. Multiplying this figure by three would give an approximate membership of 450 adults. With a generally above average size family the total population of the Old Order community in the Wellesley-Mornington area could easily total more than double the number of baptized members.

Observations And Trends

Although all Old Order congregations still use the German language in their worship services, English is the predominant language in home and community. One of the problems facing these people at the moment, and will even more so in the immediate future, is how to maintain the German language. Since they have a few of their own elementary schools, German can be taught. However, not all the Old Order children go to their own private schools, and secondly, even though German is taught, the fact that English is the language in general use will make it difficult to maintain German in the worship services. Most of the literature produced by Pathway Publishers, an Amish establishment in Aylmer, Ontario, is in the English language. It would appear that a change of language in worship is inevitable in the not too distant future.

Another question invariably raised is how long the Old Order Amish can successfully continue their outmoded way of life in our modern society. While the author claims no prophetic powers he sees no danger of the demise of the Amish community. Amish ways are built on deep religious convictions strengthened by centuries of tradition. Furthermore, Amish life and society provide a very stable and secure social matrix from which to extricate oneself becomes a painful experience. The Amish way of life provides social security from the cradle to the grave without government assistance.

This is not to say that no Amish ever leave the faith of their fathers. Many have left in the past and others will no doubt continue to do so. This trend is more prevalent among the more progressive groups than it is among the Old Order people. Very few from the latter group leave directly for the "world," although such exceptions do occur. More frequently they join a more progressive group of Amish and then occasionally keep on moving up and out of the Mennonite family altogether. Although no accurate figures to substantiate the claim are available, it is fairly obvious that percentage-wise the Old Order Amish have been increasing faster numerically than the more progressive groups during the last 30 years.

The Old Order Amish have been remarkably successful in withstanding outward change and in maintaining most of the traditional Amish ideals and practices. They have found it just as difficult, however, as the rest to maintain a true spirituality and untarnished motives. Unfortunately, some carnal vices have marred their fellowship. The excessive use of alcoholic beverages is a common problem among both the older and younger people. Unchristian attitudes and actions arising out of differences manifest themselves only too frequently. With their strict discipline and very little allowance for deviation from prescribed practices it is difficult to determine whether actions spring from true love of God or mere fear of man. It is entirely possible that submission to the Amish way of life may be motivated by a selfish craving for social security rather than by a genuine commitment of faith. Tradition, rather than faith, can easily become the dominating motivation.

Looking at the brighter side, there is increasing evidence that the Amish are becoming more conscious of the pitfalls peculiar to their society. The success of the Old Order Amish publishing venture in Aylmer, Ontario, with its increasing output of Christian literature augurs well for a more intelligent grasp of their heritage and faith. The cross-fertilization of ideas which this literature makes possible among Amish settlements in the United States and Canada, is bound to have its effect for good. The pace of change will continue to be slow, but changes have taken place and will no doubt continue, hopefully for the better.

The Beachy Amish

The Beachy Amish designation originated in Pennsylvania in the late 1920s after a division in an Old Order congregation in that state. The name was derived from the bishop of the congregation — Moses M. Beachy. There is no formal organization uniting Beachy Amish congregations. They simply represent a number of congregations with similar beliefs and practices. Generally speaking they assume a half-way position between the Old Order and so-called Church Amish.

The two congregations in Ontario usually classified as Beachy Amish are the Nafziger and Lichti churches. Reference to the origin of these two congregations was made earlier in chapter five. Both of these congregations had their beginning quite some time before the beginning of the Beachy Amish in the United States.

The Nafziger group had its beginning in 1903 and the Lichti, or Cedar Grove, congregation in 1911. Both were named after the bishops who headed the more conservative element in the

Mornington and Wellesley Township Amish congregations. The two congregations built meeting houses shortly after their formation but otherwise maintained practically all the older practices and traditions. Since that time, however, they have made more changes than the Old Order churches. Modern farm machinery has been acceptable almost from the beginning. Telephones and automobiles have been permitted since 1946. While the group's conservatism is evident in the color of their cars (usually black) it is not so evident in the more expensive models frequently found among them. Homes of members, particularly middle aged and younger people, usually display modern decor and furnishings. In the area of dress and grooming there have not been as many changes but a very noticeable difference exists in comparison to the Old Order Amish. The younger women wear more colorful dresses, coats rather than shawls, and prayer caps rather than veils. The men wear their hair shorter and beards are more severely trimmed.

Despite this modernization in material things, both congregations have maintained most of the older religious traditions and practices. German is still the predominant language of worship although some English is now used by some of the ministers. The **Ausbund** hymnal is used in regular Sunday morning worship. Sunday evening hymn-sings, held alternately in the two congregations, use the **Lieder Und Melodien** and **Church and Sunday School** hymnals. The young people also use the **Christian Hymnal,** an all-English song book published by the Church of God in Christ Mennonites. The Lichti congregation has a bi-weekly Bible study with members from the Nafziger church also attending. Neither church has Sunday school or any other church-sponsored activity. The young people have recently had some missionary projects. A missions emphasis, evident in recent years, is at least partly the result of the influence of a more progressive element among the Old Order Amish of the United States.

One of the new developments referred to in the previous chapter is the increased output of literature by, and for, the Old Order and Beachy Amish. The older paper, Herald der Wahrheit (Herald of Truth), has been widely read for a long time. Possibly the most popular magazine currently is the Budget an Ohio-based weekly paper giving Amish news and views in typical newspaper style. Gaining in popularity are periodicals published by Pathway Publishers in Aylmer, Ontario. The Blackboard Bulletin specializes in parochial school issues, and Family Life caters to interests indicated by its title. Calvary Messenger, a comparatively new paper published by the Beachy Amish in the United States, is also being read by members of the Nafziger and Lichti congregations. As suggested earlier, this new literary activity provides real potential for renewal among Old Order and Conservative groups.

A number of areas of tension have arisen in both congregations in the last number of years. One of these was related to the requirement that young married men must wear beards. Others included more directly church-related issues: the use of English in worship services, Sunday school, more evening services, and a more progressive church program generally. Until the last several years the more aggressive members, and those wanting more personal freedom, usually left the congregations to join one of the conference churches. Sometimes this became merely one step into the "world" as they moved on out and into other Protestant, or even Catholic churches. Lately, however, possibly because of the increasing modernization of the conference churches, a number of members from these two groups have formed a new congregation, another half-way step between the Beachy Amish and the conference churches. The particulars of this group will be discussed later.

The Mornington, or Nafziger congregation numbers about 170 adult members and continues to worship in its original meeting house built in 1904. This is the only one of the early meeting houses built by the Amish in Ontario that remains virtually intact. It is a unique replica of a by-gone age and architectural design. The congregation is without a resident bishop since Moses Nafziger passed away several years ago. Serving as ministers are Lorne Schmidt, Leonard Jantzi, and Melvin Roes. Aaron N. Jantzi is the deacon.

The Cedar Grove congregation numbers nearly 200 adult members and is in charge of Bishop Samuel Roth with Noah Gerber and Melvin Jantzi serving as ministers. John L. Zehr is deacon. The congregation built a new meeting house in 1963. Although a very simple structure it does have a full basement, faces the road longitudinally, in contrast to the older structure, and is patterned after more recent designs.

Salem Fellowship

Salem Fellowship is made up primarily of people from the Nafziger and Lichti congregations who wanted a more aggressive church program, as indicated earlier. Organization of the congregation took place in 1969. The group purchased a former Anglican church building in Elma township, about five miles northwest of Milverton. Since that time an addition has been built to provide more adequate space for Sunday school and related activities. Leaders of the congregation are Lorne Steckley, ordained minister in 1969, and Mervin L. Kuepfer, ordained deacon in 1970. Allen Slabaugh, a bishop from Nappanee, Indiana, assisted in organizing the congregation and performs bishop duties when his services are required.

The adult membership is around 20 persons with the actual attendance averaging about 45 at regular worship services. The congregation has weekly worship services and Sunday school. Sunday school literature is acquired from Rod and Staff Publishers who came into being as a result of a conservative-oriented schism in the Mennonite Church in Canada and the United States in the late 1950s. Sunday evening services, a regular feature, vary considerably in structure and content. Young people of the congregation frequently fellowship with another congregation in Milverton taking a similar stance. Services are conducted in the English language. The **Christian Hymnal,** an all-English song book, is used in all worship services.

Bethel Conservative Congregation

Bethel Conservative congregation came into being as a result of a division in the Riverdale congregation in 1956. Valentine Nafziger, then bishop of the congregation, insisted on stricter regulations, particularly related to dress, than were practised by the other churches in the Amish conference at the time. The group continues to require the so-called regulation dress of the Mennonite church which came to Ontario with the revival movement at the turn of the century. This type of dress was never widely accepted by the Amish in Ontario, and was never required in the conference churches. Shortly after the division in Millbank a similar movement in some Mennonite congregations in Ontario resulted in a number of families from that conference joining the new Bethel congregation. Several other new congregations primarily of Mennonite background but drawing a few Amish families as well, were also formed about this time.

The Conservative Mennonite Church, the name adopted by the congregation following the division, built a new structure about a mile east of the Riverdale church in 1957. By 1970 the membership had reached nearly 100. However, a division in the congregation that year resulted in over half of the members leaving to form another group. Current adult membership is 38 with regular attendance, counting children and adults, considerably higher.

The distinguishing feature of the Conservative congregation as it relates to the conference churches is its emphasis on so-called plain clothes and a generally more conservative Mennonite outlook. While congregational life and activities are very similar the literature used reflects the conservative emphasis. Sunday school material was for a time acquired from Rod and Staff Publishers but more recently is purchased from the Sword and Trumpet Publishers of Virginia. Songbooks used are the older edition of the **Mennonite Hymnal** and **Life Songs** No. 2.

Valentine Nafziger has continued as bishop of the congregation except for a brief period of time in the late sixties when he was deprived of his prerogatives over an alleged moral indiscretion. It was over the dissatisfaction with the handling of this matter that a division in the congregation occurred in 1970. Because of his age and failing health, Nafziger resigned his office in 1972. Kenneth Brenneman, Nafziger's son-in-law, was ordained to succeed him as bishop of the congregation. Both Brenneman and his father-in-law have served extensively in other like-minded congregations in the United States and Canada. In 1971 Orval Baer was ordained to serve the Bethel congregation.

Milverton Conservative Fellowship

The Milverton Conservative Mennonite congregation was formed as a result of the division of the Bethel congregation referred to above. The group purchased a former United Church of Canada building in Milverton following the 1970 division. The membership is about 70 with regular Sunday attendance exceeding 100.

The congregation's activities are quite similar to those of other congregations discussed in this chapter. Sunday school literature is acquired from Rod and Staff Publishers; the **Christian Hymnal** as well as other conservative Mennonite literature is used. There is some cooperation with the Salem Fellowship group.

Ralph Gerber, ordained deacon by the Bethel congregation in 1962 was the only ordained man in the group which left Bethel in 1970. Consequently, Bishop Andrew Stutzman of Ohio assisted in organizing the new congregation. David

Fischer and Daniel Gascho were ordained as ministers. Gerber continues as deacon while Stutzman has bishop oversight of the congregation.

Conservatives in British Columbia

During the 1960s three congregations, composed of people of Amish and Mennonite background, were established in Canada's most westerly province. First ordination of ministers to serve in the first congregation at McBride, British Columbia, was performed during a Bible conference held at the Bethel Conservative Mennonite church near Millbank. Valentine Nafziger, bishop of the Bethel group and formerly of the Amish congregation in Millbank, served as the bishop of the British Columbia congregation for four years. The two other congregations in the province are located at Crescent Spur and Dunster.

All of the congregations in B.C. are located approximately due west of Edmonton, Alberta, in the eastern part of British Columbia. The area is virgin territory with most of it requiring bush clearing before cropping can begin. Most of the Amish located there are from the United States although a few were originally from Ontario. Once again it is an attempt to get away from the allurements of the "world". Each of the congregations is comparatively small, McBride being the largest with approximately 50 members.

Maple Grove Congregation

In the previous chapter an account was given of the division in the East Zorra church which gave birth to the Maple Grove congregation. This represents the most recent division in any of the Western Ontario Conference churches. Taking a somewhat similar conservative stand as the congregations above, the group is more traditionally Amish than the other conservative congregations discussed earlier. The group began meeting separately in 1966 with Daniel Wagler, former minister in East Zorra, as leader. With the assistance of bishops from the Conservative Mennonite Conference in the United States the congregation in 1969 chose and ordained two younger men to the ministry. The two were Oliver Yantzi and Maurice Witzel. Wagler, however, also continues to serve. Adult membership is 63 with about 40 children, making a total population of about 100.

Following the division the group purchased a former public

elementary school located on the 17th Line of East Zorra Township. Since then an addition has been built to provide more space for Sunday school and other activities. The building is located a few miles north of the Cassel church.

Church activities are limited to Sunday morning and evening services, except for occasional special meetings with guest speakers. In the junior department of the Sunday school Rod and Staff literature is used. The adult classes use Sword and Trumpet quarterlies. The congregation has now voted to acquire the **Christian Hymnal,** published by the Church of God in Christ Mennonites. The women of the church meet each month for a sewing fellowship meeting.

This concludes the survey of the original Old Order and other more conservative congregations in Ontario. It is interesting to note that new congregations springing from the more conservative groups tend to be more liberal and aggressive, whereas those hailing from the more progressive congregations are invariably more conservative. The tensions which gave rise to all of the foregoing divisions are constantly present in every congregation to a greater or lesser degree. Division results only when strong leadership is present in both camps. Consequently, personality conflicts rather than differences in substance are the real cause of division. This is not to deny that real differences exist. It is saying, however, that differences are secondary, not primary, causes of division.

32-33. Abraham Gingerich, who was enterprising and progressive enough to build his own waterwheel and electrical plant in his earlier years, ***witnessed his own creation being replaced by Ontario Hydro.***

12 The Ever-Changing New Order

"Today is not yesterday. We ourselves change. How then, can our works and thoughts, if they are always to be the fittest, continue always the same. Change, indeed, is painful, yet ever needful; and if memory have its force and worth, so also has hope."
— Carlyle

While the ideal of the Old Order has been to preserve everything as it was in the beginning, the philosophy of Carlyle quoted above more nearly states the sentiments guiding the New Order. Obviously the titles of this and the preceding chapter are overstated. Yet there is an element of truth in each, and from merely outward appearances they seem quite apropos. The Old Order, as we noticed, is by no means changeless. And conversely, even though the New Order appears to have lost almost all of its Amish identity, it is not without some strong affinity with the Old Order.

The New Order still bases its actions squarely on the scriptures, although it interprets and applies them in new ways. The concept of discipleship has issued in an emphasis on service and witness reflected in the mission-service projects referred to earlier. The emphasis on humility and on non-materialistic values is still evident in a generally modest consumption of goods, and ownership. Even though the brotherhood concept has been shorn of some of its outward expressions by the welfare state it is by no means dead. Participation in the Fire and Storm Aid Union, response to tragedy, both within and without the brotherhood, still evokes a quick response of concrete action. These are at least a few of the positive elements of the heritage that remains despite outward changes. But let us look again at some of the changes that have come to the majority of the Amish in the last 50 years.

Worship

There were comparatively few changes in the congregational life of the Amish churches in Ontario before 1920. The major ones which did take place were discussed in a previous chapter and were specifically, a change from worship services in homes to meeting houses. This change also eliminated the traditional fellowship meal following the bi-weekly worship service. Around the turn of the century Sunday schools became a part of congregational activity. These were often held alternately with the worship service which made for weekly, rather than bi-weekly services. One other significant change before 1920 was the adoption of new hymnals and faster tunes than were used with the **Ausbund.** Aside from these few changes congregational life continued essentially the same till the twenties.

One of the new things which happened in the twenties, with only rare exceptions before that, were protracted evening meetings. While such meetings had been held in the Blake church in 1908, the resulting division probably did much to slow down acceptance of the innovation. The East Zorra congregation probably had more of these meetings in the twenties and early thirties than any other congregation in the conference. A number of ministers from the United States including John Mast, Jonas Yoder, Sam Greaser and Michael Zehr held meetings in Ontario. C. F. Derstine, a bishop of First Mennonite Church in Kitchener, also held meetings in the early thirties in a number of congregations. Also in the thirties Aaron Mast from Pennsylvania and B. B. King from Ohio held similar revival meetings in the province. The minister who had major influence through evangelistic meetings during the thirties and forties was Nelson Litwiller, the first seminary-trained Amishman from Ontario, who went to South America as a missionary in 1925. Litwiller invariably had several such series of meetings while home on furlough from Argentina.

Another innovation in the twenties was the introduction of Sunday school lesson quarterlies. Previously studies were primarily taken from the New Testament in chapter and book studies. With the use of lesson quarterlies soon also came the use, particularly by the young people, of the English language. A conference resolution in 1929 gave the first official recognition and encouragement to the use of English in the teaching program of the church. Jacob R. Bender of East Zorra and Peter Nafziger from Wilmot were probably the first ministers in the conference to preach in English — sometime in the thirties. However, the German language was continued in most congregations during the thirties and in some cases to the early fifties. The extent of the change in language is best illustrated by the change in hymn books in the late thirties. The hymn book in use since about 1915 had an appendix of English hymns; the hymnal adopted now relegated German hymns to the appendix.

Also slowly changing during these years was the length of the worship service. Sunday school was switched to precede the worship service; consequently, sermons became shorter and soon there was no time left for testimonies to preacher's message by the other ministers present. The same was true of the counsel meeting and communion service. Instead of lasting four to five hours these services were reduced to two or three hours, and still later to an hour and a half and today, in most cases, to no longer than a regular worship service.

Many other smaller changes have occurred in worship during these years. Offerings previously were held only when some specific need arose; now they are a regular feature of each worship service. In more recent times there is more congregational participation through the use of antiphonal, unison, or responsive readings, sharing sessions following the sermon, or an occasional service conducted by the youth of the church. While the "Conference Amish" worship service of today is still non-liturgical, it is quite similar to any in the Protestant free church tradition.

The Sunday school, which in the writer's view has played a very important role in the past, seems to have lost much of its dynamic. This is a common phenomenon in many churches. The cutting edge of the church has moved to other areas. On the other hand the church's study hour in some ways has been used creatively. It has been employed to discuss current issues facing the church, or as a prelude to decisions and action in making changes in practice relating to church leadership, the communion service, baptism, and others. Some congregations use the Sunday school hour for discussion of the minister's sermon, attempting in this way to make the brotherhood of the church more practical. This is in line with the earlier tradition of inviting lay response to the message.

Other attempts at revitalizing the institution include the offering of other courses of study as options to the Uniform Lessons series. Perhaps one of the reasons the Sunday school has lost its leadership role is because it has fallen into a rut and instead of being an innovator it tends to be a defender of the status quo. It needs to be more flexible than in the past, with its most urgent need being leadership with vision and courage to venture in new directions.

Organization

Organizationally there has been a tremendous change since 1920. With the increase in activity has come an increase in organization. It was not until the fifties and sixties that these changes affected the main congregational structure. Before this the ordained men formed a council which was the organizational backbone of every church. There were Sunday school superintendents, young people's Bible meeting committee members, and literary societies before the fifties but these were limited to their own little spheres. During the fifties and sixties most congregations organized church councils to facilitate the coordination of the many activities and also to provide a more democratic church government. During the last decade congregations have been moving in the direction of a one pastor system, instead of multiple ordained ministry, further necessitating church councils.

Another development originating in the late sixties was the appointment of elders as pastors' assistants. This has taken place in most congregations where there is only one minister. These men also serve as a more intimate counselling body for the pastor, as well as assisting in any other way the pastor may request, including preaching. In most such cases an older and a younger man have deliberately been chosen to give the ministerial council the best possible age representation. There are, however, a number of congregations which still have more than one ordained man and so have no elders. In most cases elders are appointed for a three or four-year term with privilege of reappointment.

There are also several deacons left in the conference but no new ones are being ordained. The same holds true for bishops. No bishops have been defrocked; they have simply become unnecessary since all ministers have been given the privilege of performing all the church's ordinances. There are presently, in the Western Ontario Conference, no active bishops in the traditional sense of that office. The conference executive committee together with the conference minister assume responsibility for assisting congregations in need of leadership.

A further change in leadership has been the increasing number of seminary-trained men serving in the ministry. While there is still, among some older and a few younger people, a considerable feeling against formal education for ministers, the need for seminary training is generally recognized. Only 20 years ago there were no seminary trained men in the conference. Currently about half of the pastors have had at least some formal theological training. There are, however, no educational requirements for the ministry. A reading, group sharing, study course has been set up for congregational leaders. The objectives of the program are stated as threefold: to develop leadership abilities in the context of the Christian brotherhood, a continuing education program for ministers and laymen, and to recruit people for the ministry of the Christian church. The reading is designed to increase the biblical-theological and practical knowledge of the participants. The group sharing experience is intended to deepen self-understanding and facilitate teamwork among leaders of each congregation.

Twenty years ago there was practically no systematic financial support for ministers in any of the congregations in the conference. This too has changed. The majority of churches now support their pastors. However, only a few have a full time, fully supported pastor. While the changes in this area, set against the background of a typical Amish emphasis on a non-professional and non-salaried ministry, appear to be very slow, they have, in fact, been comparatively rapid. Obviously the contemporary trend is toward a trained and supported ministry, although a few congregations are moving in the direction of a team-ministry. With more formally-educated laymen of various professions in the church this option is a live possibility and certainly compatible with Amish tradition.

Another very obvious change relative to church polity is in the matter of church discipline. Automatic excommunication for certain transgressions is no longer practised. If practised at all, excommunication is used only against those who refuse to confess their guilt. The ban, in the strict Amish sense, is no longer practised. In most cases, confession for public sin before the entire congregation is still required. Although "counsel meeting" before the communion service is still used to urge self-examination, denial of communion is no longer employed as a disciplinary measure. Instead of explicitly defined rules and regulations and an enforced conformity, considerable personal liberty is allowed while general principles are stressed.

While numerous factors have contributed to this change in stance on church discipline, two seem to be outstanding. One is a reaction to the inconsistencies generated by a rather legalistic application of some favorite New Testament passages. Like most reactions it has tended to swing the church into the opposite extreme where every man does that which is right in his own eyes. A more positive reason for the change has been a serious attempt to interpret and apply, in light of the entire New Testament, the specific passages of scripture used previously. Whether the attempt to uphold personal liberty and responsibility will in the long run result in a more dynamic church and brotherhood remains to be seen.

Increased Activity

Activities, particularly in the last 20 years, have been multiplied in most congregations. Women's sewing circles have been operating since the 1920s, but only in the last ten to 20 years have they become part of the broader Mennonite Women's Missionary and Service Commission (W.M.S.C.). In Ontario, the women of the Western (Amish) and Mennonite (Old) conferences cooperate in one provincial organization. Girls' work is carried on for various age levels. "Wayfarers" is the organization attempting to meet the needs of elementary school age girls. Probably most church councils now have one or more female members. Women also serve as song leaders, chorus directors, Sunday school teachers, and superintendents of pre-school Sunday school departments. Otherwise, church leadership is still very much men's domain. While the gains in this area again seem small they have been faster in the last 20 years than in most churches because of the more traditional outlook of the Amish in the twenties and thirties.

Married couples' fellowships, which attempt to provide a program suited to younger married couples with children, have organized in many congregations. Although strong family ties have been characteristic of the Amish, as in all of Mennonite culture, the more progressive, who have been swept into the mainstream culture of our time, are experiencing some of the fragmentation of family life that is prevalent in today's society. Married couples' groups tend to foster family togetherness as well as family sharing. A regular annual weekend at Hidden Acres Camp in North Easthope Township is usually well attended and provides informal fellowship for whole families, together with inspiration and opportunity for discussion of problems, issues, and challenges facing the family.

There are usually few special activities for men on the congregational level. Farm, business, and community involvement keep most of them fully occupied. Missionary projects, referred to elsewhere, are one avenue of service and fellowship in which men participate to some degree. A boys' program for elementary age — known as Torchbearers — is similar to Boy Scouts. Older young people's activities are programmed through the Mennonite Youth Fellowship (MYF). Usually one or two married couples are appointed as sponsors to the congregational organization. The program attempts to keep a balance between faith (Bible study, worship, etc.), serving (doing things for others, community, church), and fellowship (social gatherings, sports, etc.)

Much of the increased activity in the congregation in the last 50 years may well be the result of an injection of new spiritual life. Admittedly, other factors have also played an important role; the influence of the larger society, the theology and practice of other denominatons, to mention only a few, have helped to bring about the transformation which has taken place. It is obvious, on the other hand, that mere activity does not take the place of genuine in-depth Christian experience and understanding. One of the greatest needs in the Western Ontario Mennonite Conference and its congregations at present is a more thorough and comprehensive biblical knowledge, and an understanding of the true significance of the Anabaptist heritage. It is also evident from congregational histories that the vitality of any church is dependent largely on its leadership, both lay and ordained. Strong leadership of the right kind has been the secret of progress and unity, but strong leadership, both ordained or lay, has also been at the root of many divisions which have occurred in the last 100 years of Amish history in Ontario.

A New Piety

Not only has there been an outward transformation, evidenced by many clearly visible changes, but there have also been tremendous inner changes. These changes have come as a result of a changing emphasis brought about largely by a pietistic, revivalistic influence of the past 100, and more particularly, the past 50 years. There was already some pietistic influence in Europe. Historians and theologians in the past three decades have pointed out the source of some of these influences. Particularly illuminating is a work called **Mennonite Piety through the Centuries** by Robert Friedmann.

One of the more obvious changes brought by the pietist influence has been the acceptance of total abstinence in the use of tobacco and alcohol. The switch came partly as a reaction against abuse but more specifically as a result of the typical Protestant holiness movement. Perhaps less obvious is the separation between the so-called secular and sacred. This is most evident in the attitude of contemporary older people who find it hard to accept certain activities carried on in the church buildings, especially by young people. With the acceptance of meeting houses apparently also came the typical "church" theology that makes a church building more "sacred" than a house or barn. In the traditional Amish sense sacredness resided in the people, not the building. In early days the fellowship meal following the worship service was an integral part of the worship experience; later eating in the church was wrong. It became a secular activity which was out of place in the "spiritual" atmosphere of a church building. One could go on multiplying examples of how slowly and insiduously some of these concepts which the Anabaptists had rejected came back through the door of modern pietism.

Nevertheless, strange as it may seem, some of these same influences brought back to the Amish some of the more biblical concepts lost through centuries of tradition. An example is the emphasis on a conversion experience. Being as they were a simple, Bible believing church, the new birth had always been taught, although more as a command than an experience. Anbaptism was obedience-centered rather than the experience-centeredness typical of pietism and modern American revivalism. The danger of the obedience-centered emphasis is that it tends to degenerate to a moralistic legalism, a pitfall the Amish did not escape. Consequently, the emphasis on experience was a good corrective and brought new life and vitality into the Amish church.

All of this is not to say that the church was formerly all bad and now is all good, or vice versa. It does indicate, however, the humanness of the church and how, despite its emphasis against worldliness, it is always influenced by the world and the times in which it exists. Original Anabaptism was dynamically evangelistic whereas the Amish have been quietistic. Humility was stressed to the point where a person did not talk about his faith, religion, or experiences. Some of these attitudes have slowly changed over the years, but in this area the church is still far from the faith and practice of the fathers. The Amish, with the Mennonites, have tended to adopt some of modern revivalism's emphases and techniques but little of Anabaptism's original vision and dynamic.

As in larger Mennonitism, so also among the Amish some of the elements of the original emphasis still exist, giving uniqueness to its piety. One of the best illustrations is the combination of missions and service. Protestantism generally is divided on this point. Liberalism emphasizes service and social action while conservatism or evangelicalism stresses missions and evangelism. Although this tension also exists in Mennonite circles there is usually a fairly healthy combination. The Anabaptist emphasis on obedience and discipleship has maintained a very practical Christianity on the whole, and kept piety from its usual tenency of degenerating into a mere emotionalism. Another way in which pietism has been a corrective is by changing the Amish over-emphasis on "being" in relation to witnessing. That is, witnessing primarily by the kind of life you live as against "doing" mission work — preaching the Gospel to non-Christians or becoming involved in the needs of the community and the world. The mission-service activities recounted earlier are evidence of this change.

Another change in Amish piety is the general attitude toward God and the Christian life. This change was expressed very aptly by an older sister in the church when she said, "Die furcht is nimmy dat" (the fear of the Lord is not evident anymore). The English word "fear" does not do justice to the concept implied in the German word "furcht" as used here. Admittedly, there was an element of fear in Amish piety, but more specifically it meant awe, respect and reverence. The Amish experience of persecution in Europe flavored their concept of the Christian life as being primarily one of cross-bearing and suffering. This concept, coupled with a typical old-country emphasis on authority, made for a very sombre religious outlook. The communion service, for instance, was centered basically around the suffering of Christ. The change from this mood to a more free and joyous attitude, with a less severe God, is no doubt due to a number of factors. Certainly the times in which we live, in comparative peace and prosperity, together with a de-emphasis on authority have had their effect. Pietism, with its emphasis on experience and the joy of salvation as a present reality has played an important role in this change.

A New Outlook

A change in outlook among the Amish is not limited to personal piety, however. Perhaps even more noticeable is the new attitude toward the "world". This change was again put tersely by one person who exclaimed, "A few years ago we were told to turn our backs to the world, now we are being asked to face it!" From an emphasis on non-conformity to, and separation from the world, the Amish have arrived at an attitutde of accommodation which stresses involvement. The former position led to an exlusiveness and withdrawal which did indeed protect the church from outward, although not necessarily inward worldliness. While it kept alive some of the basic Anabaptist concepts of radical discipleship, separation, and brotherhood, because of its exclusiveness it failed to a large extent to be salt and light. And even these concepts tended to become stale and meaningless because they were too much turned in on the inner life of the church.

Evidence of a more outgoing attitude is the greater involvement by members of the Western Ontario Mennonite Conference in community affairs. This greater participation is in evidence on several levels. Reference was made earlier to political involvement by members on town and township councils. Other political involvement includes expressing the church's convictions regarding social issues of the day, e.g. capital punishment, marriage and divorce. The same trend is evident on the social level with more frequent participation in community, social and cultural events. In addition, joint services with older denominations have become quite common. Where a generation ago a member of the Amish church was automatically excommunicated when marrying a member of another denomination, today a Mennonite minister can, without censure, participate in an ecumenical wedding ceremony with a Catholic priest.

Although there is more political involvement by the more progressive element of Amish today this does not mean they have dropped the principle of separation of church and state. It means simply that they have dropped a very restricted view of that principle. The Western Ontario Conference does not have any restrictions relative to participation in such government plans as family allowance, health insurance, old age pension, etc. The Conference has also accepted government funds for the erection and operation of some of its community-serving institutions. It does not see this as a violation of the separation principle, providing the church "is not forced to down-grade its beliefs and practices in accepting the same". In the same document separation of church and state is defined "as meaning the state has no right to legislate in matters of doctrine and practice, and conversely the church has no right to enforce its doctrine on the general public through the state." The statement goes on to say that this is not to be interpreted as meaning there can be no cooperation or interaction between the church and the state. It means that neither institution should use the other for its own ends.

A New Openness

The new outlook referred to above naturally makes for a new openness toward others, acceptance of new ideas and concepts, as well as new ways of doing things. The tremendous changes which have occurred among the majority of the Amish in Ontario are ample evidence of this fact. It is typically Amish to consider anything new as evil and a threat to the faith of the fathers. This attitude has changed greatly except among the Old Order and conservative groups. There exists, in fact, the danger of going to the opposite extreme.

With most of the old exclusive sanctions gone and the

impact made by the mass media the openness presents some real threats. There is a fairly wide-spread recognition that no particular magic rests in any denominational name, either Amish or Mennonite, or any other for that matter. The danger is that there may be a failure to recognize some of the distinctive features of their religious heritage. We indicated earlier that some of this may already have happened in the area of giving concrete expression to the brotherhood concept of the church.

With the proliferation of ideas comes the possibility of divisiveness unless there is a corresponding tolerance. There is a greatly increased tolerance although this very tolerance may permit people to adopt some intolerant ideas. Religious fundamentalism, with its narrow and dogmatic, doctrinal base, is a good example. This type of Christianity, often propounded over radio programs, has a certain appeal to Mennonites and Amish with their background of simple biblicism. On the other hand, the increasing acceptance of education on every level can lead to the opposite extreme, which is really the same problem in different garb. An intolerant and often impatient liberalism is just as detrimental to unity and true spirituality as the narrow dogmatism of fundamentalism.

On the positive side, the new openness has brought a new freedom to the fellowship of the church. The recent revised statement on church discipline is indicative of the new mood. There is currently considerable freedom in the expression of faith in the churches of the Western Ontario Conference. Many of these new freedoms are not necessarily peculiar to the Amish. They exist in many other denominations as well. But perhaps for the first time the Amish are not years behind in accepting new ideas and new ways of doing things.

The new openness also holds greater possibilities for the constant need for renewal in the church. If, however, a denomination has a closed system of beliefs and practices, the chances of renewal are greatly lessened. A current example is the charismatic movement. In the past, members who became involved in similar experiences either left the church or were excommunicated. Today this is no longer necessarily the case. There are scores of people in the churches of the conference who have experienced the so-called baptism of the Holy Spirit together with some of the gifts of the Spirit as outlined in the New Testament. Other avenues to renewal — such as the small group movement, retreats, celebrations, etc. — although accepted with some reservations, are permitted and even encouraged. While openness does not by any means guarantee renewal, renewal seldom happens without it.

The foregoing is at least a partial glimpse of the change in the religious life of the Amish in Ontario. Whether these changes have been good or bad depends on the criteria used to evaluate them. In the human situation it is always a mixture of both. Time usually gives a partial answer, although the final judgment is reserved for the judge of all the earth.

Achieving Goals

The Amish came to Canada seeking freedom from religious, political, and economic oppression. For several hundred years they had been forced to migrate on numerous occasions. There were times when they experienced brief periods of peace and freedom, although often these were of short duration till once again they were compelled to find a new haven. Little wonder that the prospect of purchasing their own land, instead of being only tenants always at the mercy of landlords, plus the promise of military exemption, should bring hundreds of Amish pioneers to North America.

With few exceptions the Amish found in Canada the freedom and peace for which they had sought so long. From the time they arrived in 1822 until 1849, Canadian law required the payment of fines in lieu of military service; a requirement most of them were familiar with from their experience in Europe. The only other penalties imposed for the privilege of military exemption were the denial of the right to vote during the two world wars and the performing of alternate work of national importance during World War II for a minimum wage of 50 cents per day. The remaining portion of the wages earned by the young men of conscription age went to the Canadian Red Cross.

Although freedom from physical want was not easily attained in early pioneer days, they were at no time forced, as in Europe, to abandon the hard earned fruits of their labour. Naturally, their fortunes fluctuated with the general economy of the country and quite a number sought greener pastures during the depression of the late nineteenth century. Since that time, except for the depression of the early 1930s, the economic prosperity, the peace and plenty of the last three-quarter century would have been beyond the fondest dreams of the forefathers. The descendants of these poor but hearty pioneers are indeed reaping the fruits, not only of this land we call Canada, but also of the faith, courage and hard work of their ancestors. Few people have ever "had it so good" in material things and religious freedom.

Quite aside from exemption from military service, the Amish of Canada have experienced religious freedom in every other way as well. Removed from the religious partisanship which Europe inherited from the Reformation, and surrounded by others of similar cultural traditions who also sought simple freedom from both religious and political oppression, the Amish found ideal conditions to worship and live according to their beliefs. As indicated in the first chapter of this book, North America is the only place the Amish have continued as a distinct group. While the reasons for this are no doubt many, the religious tolerance and freedom in the new world must be considered a significant factor. Gratefulness for this freedom and petitions for those in authority were invariably present in the worship and prayers of the forefathers, and the same is still true today.

The Amish have played a significant role in the settlement and development of a number of townships in midwestern Ontario. In the last 150 years they have helped turn a wilderness into one of the most productive areas of the continent. Although this was not the main purpose of their coming to this country, it is germane to their philosophy of life to build rather than destroy, to live and let live. That they have achieved these goals is not alone to their credit. Their immediate neighbors, the people of Canada and its representative government, also share in the honors.

Crucial Failures

Being as human as everybody else the Amish also failed to achieve some of their goals. Perhaps their greatest shortcoming is the failure to achieve the in-group harmony which their faith idealizes. The toleration they have asked for in the larger society they have not always been willing to grant each other; the divisions which have occurred in the Canadian brotherhood reveal this only too clearly. While they have lived in comparative peace in the world, they have often failed to achieve peace in the church. Tension between the more progressive and the more conservative elements in the Amish community have been a root cause of the divisions in the brotherhood, divisions which have marred their Christian testimony.

Reference was made earlier that during the first 50 or more years of their sojourn in Canada there was not the cultural gap between the Amish and the rest of society that there is today. We have intimated that at least part of the reason for this insistence on old ways and customs was the failure to distinguish between the faith and the culture of the forefathers. While we do not question the motive of the Old Order Amish in maintaining 16th century ways, we do question the efficacy of the method. Tradition is not necessarily evil although it has the potential to stifle and bind people. Outward forms are kept easily enough even after the inner dynamic which created them is lost. Although free to practise their faith unhindered, the Old Order Amish of Canada may be bound in a tradition as stifling as the one their forefathers died to be saved from in 16th century Europe. This should not be interpreted as meaning that the Old Order Amish have nothing but form. It is simply trying to recognize the danger of equating genuine faith with a given form.

The more progressive element of the Amish community can hardly be accused of being bound by tradition, since they have, in 50 years lost most of the outward forms of their tradition. While the Old Order may be in danger of being bound by the past, the New Order may be in danger of becoming enslaved to the fads, fashions, and value system of the contemporary materialistic American society. There is danger also in assuming that the intense activity and greater involvement of the more progressive group automatically spells greater affinity with the faith and spiritual dynamic of their Anabaptist forefathers. Genuine freedom does not issue automatically from any lifestyle or political system, nor is it precluded from any. Both Old and New Orders have failed to achieve that inner spiritual freedom necessary to serve both God and their fellowmen to the utmost.

The Future

In an earlier chapter we indicated that there is no danger of the Old Order Amish disappearing from the Canadian scene. In fact the recent Amish immigration from the United States indicates quite the opposite. At the moment there is no reason to believe that they will not be able to maintain their traditional lifestyle and culture. Recent government action exempting the Amish from participation in its compulsory social security plan, plus the current Canadian emphasis on maintaining the cultural distinctiveness of its various people provide new hope for the Amish of Ontario.

A more unpredictable facet of Amish life is the divisiveness which has been so evident the last 100 years. A few people in virtually every generation are convinced that all fruther changes are evil and try to halt them by starting yet another intermediate group. The more conservative groups of the present will no doubt continue for a long time, although they invariably change faster than the Old Order groups. The writer does not see any new such groups on the immediate horizon. Hopefully, one of these times the lessons of history will be learned so that Christian forbearance will be shown and great harmony displayed despite differing convictions and understanding.

As for the largest segment of the Amish community in Ontario, comprising the 16 congregations of the Western Ontario Mennonite Conference, they too will continue as a separate entity for the foreseeable future. Although they have dropped not only the name but most of the distinctive Amish beliefs and practices, they still possess some of the characteristics inherited from their forefathers. They will probably continue to cooperate more closely with other Mennonite groups in Ontario and hopefully make an increasing contribution to the church at large as well as to the communities in which they live.

The story of the Amish of Canada is one of a common human struggle to survive, to live up to an ideal, to preserve a past and build for a better future. We humbly acknowledge our indebtedness to those who have gone before and dedicate ourselves anew to continue in their footsteps.

34. The Nithview old people's home for 96 persons was opened at New Hamburg as a project of the Western Ontario Mennonite Conference in 1972.

35. A modern Amish Mennonite farm in Perth County.

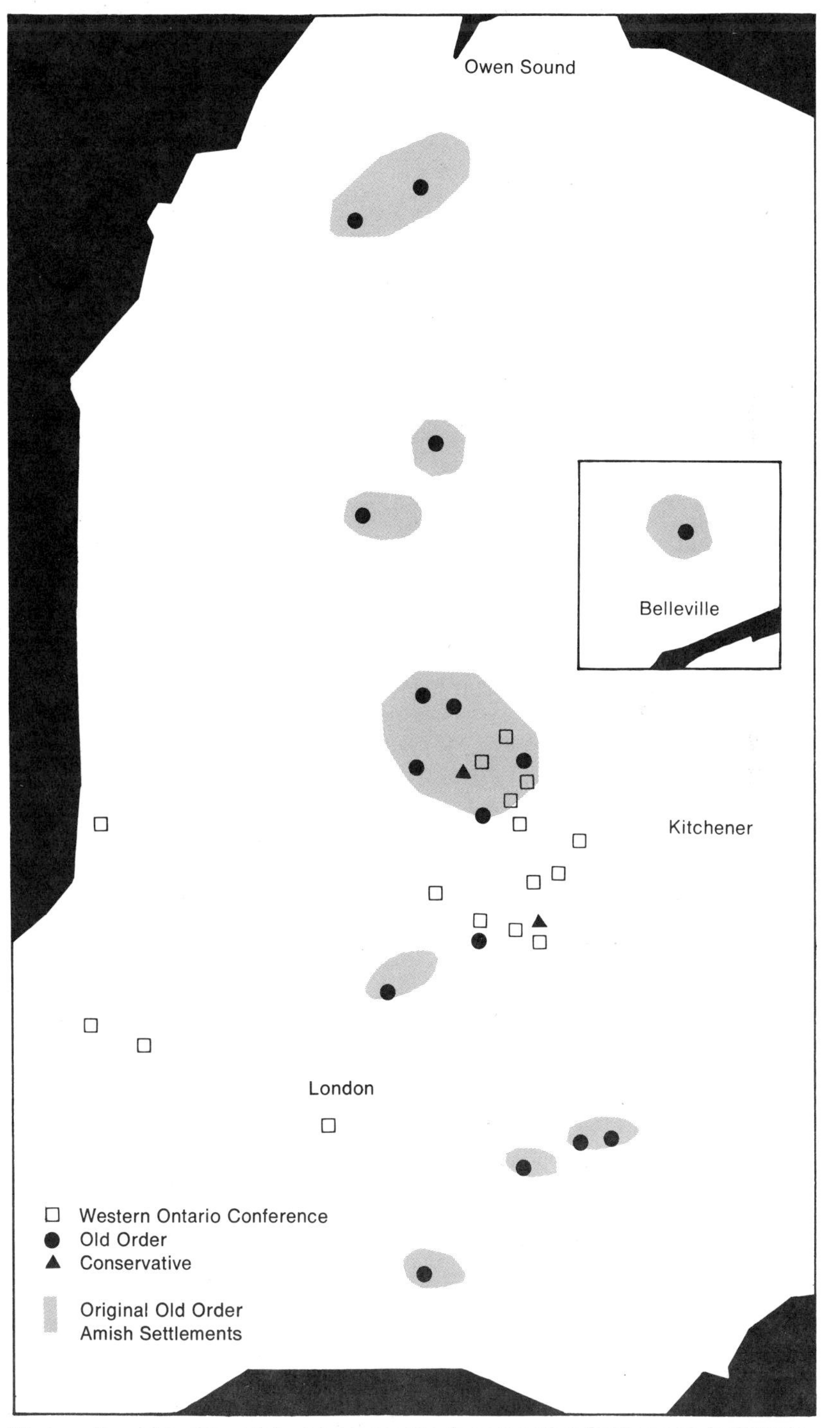

36. Location of Amish and Amish-Mennonite Congregation-Settlements in Ontario.

Bibliography

A. **Books**

Burkholder, L. J., **A Brief History of the Mennonites of Ontario,** Livingston Press Limited, 1935.

Friedmann, Robert, **Mennonite Piety Through the Centuries,** Mennonite Publishing House, 1949.

Mast, John B., **The Letters of the Amish Division,** Mennonite Publishing House, Scottdale, Pa., 1950.

Smith, C. Henry, **The Mennonites of America,** Mennonite Publishing House, 1909.

Wenger, John C., **Glimpses of Mennonite History and Doctrine,** Second edition. Herald Press, Scottdale, Pa., 1947.

Hostetler, John A., **Amish Society.** The John Hopkins Press, Baltimore, 1963.

Mennonite Encyclopedia, The (4 volumes) Mennonite Publishing House, Scottdale, Pa., 1955.

B. **Unpublished Papers and Documents**

Steinman, Gascho, and miscellaneous Amish papers in Archives of Mennonite Church, Goshen, Indiana, U.S.A.

Wilmot Township Survey and Settlement documents, Public Archives of Canada, Ottawa.

Wilmot Papers, Provincial Archives, Toronto, Ontario.

Miscellaneous Papers and Records of the Ontario Amish, Conrad Grebel College Archives, Waterloo, Ontario.

C. **Unpublished Research Papers**

Conrad Grebel College Archives

Roth, Lorraine, **A History of the East Zorra Amish Mennonite church.**

Bender, Kenneth, **A History of the Wilmot Congregation,** Eastern Mennonite College, May, 1958.

Stoll, Joseph, **Recent Amish Immigration to Ontario,** Mennonite Historical Society of Ontario, October, 1966.

Congregations and Ordained Leaders

Western Ontario Mennonite Conference

1. Wilmot (1824-1972)

   Joseph Goldschmidt (1796-1876)

   Ordained minister in 1824 by John Stoltzfus in Pennsylvania to serve in Wilmot. Moved to Ohio in 1831.

   John Brenneman

   Ordained minister in 1824, to serve with Goldschmidt in Wilmot.

Jacob Kropf

Ordained deacon in 1824, to serve with men above in Wilmot.

Peter Nafziger

Ordained bishop in Europe, came to Wilmot in 1826, served till he left for Ohio in 1831.

Christian Steinman

Ordained also in Europe, came to Wilmot in 1826.

John Oesch (1792-1850)

Ordained: minister in 1829; bishop in 1834. Moved to Huron County in 1849.

Christian Fahrni

Ordained minister in 1829, moved to Ohio in 1831.

Rudolph Roth (1798-1853)

Ordained: minister in 1835; bishop in 1843. Joined Reformed Mennonites in 1850.

Peter Litwiller (1809-1878)

Ordained: minister 1845; bishop 1850

Jacob Gardner

Ordained minister in 1845; also left Amish to join Reformed Mennonites.

Christian Miller (1806-1850)

Ordained: minister around 1830, later bishop. No exact dates available.

John Bender (1817-1874)

Ordained minister in 1847.

John Gingerich

Ordained deacon in 1847.

Christian Wagler (1810-1887)

Ordained in Europe, came to Wilmot 1848.

John Lichti (1817-1866)

Ordained deacon in 1845.

John Gascho (1830-1909)

Ordained: deacon in 1854; bishop in 1872.

Joseph Boshart (1822-1895)

Ordained minister in 1854.

Michael Kennel (1834-1898)

Ordained: deacon in 1872; minister in 1877.

Christian Wagler (Jr.) (1838-1910)

Ordained deacon in 1877.

Danlel Steinman (1831-1905)

Ordained deacon in 1872.

Christian Litwiller (1848-1924) son of bishop Peter Litwiller

Ordained: deacon in 1877; minister in 1877. (a few months later)

Daniel H. Steinman (1857-1933)

Ordained: deacon in 1893; minister in 1894 and bishop in 1898.

Christian Gascho (1857-1943)

Ordained: deacon in 1893; minister in 1894.

Peter Litwiller (1869-1930)

Ordained deacon in 1925.

Peter Nafziger (1886-1969)

Ordained: deacon in 1925, minister in 1936.

Moses O. Jantzi (1884-1965)

Ordained: deacon in 1932; minister in 1936 and bishop the same year.

Menno Wagler (1884-1958)
Ordained: deacon in 1932; minister later the same year.
Benjamin Gingerich (1883-1958)
Ordained: deacon in 1932; minister later the same year.
Michael Roth (1889-1967)
Ordained deacon in 1941.
Elmer Schwartzentruber (1909-
Ordained: deacon 1941; minister 1951.
Orland Gingerich (1920-
Ordained: minister in 1951; bishop 1954.

Following the separation of St. Agatha and Steinman's into two congregations in 1957, the following ordinations have taken place in the Steinman congregation:

Emmanuel Steinman (1899-
Ordained deacon in 1960.
Albert Zehr (1938-
Ordained minister 1965 and served here till 1971.

2. St. Agatha (1824-1972)

Originally part of the Wilmot congregation, a separate meeting house was built here in 1885, although not organized as a separate congregation until 1957 when Peter Nafziger was stationed here as pastor. The following ordinations have taken place since then:

Gerald Schwartzentruber (1933-
Ordained minister in 1960.
Allen Schwartzentruber (1903-
Ordained deacon in 1960.

3. East Zorra (1837-1972)

Nichlaus Roth (no dates available)
Ordained in Alsace.
Dr. Peter Zehr (1809-1898)
Ordained in Europe.
Daniel Schrag (1813-1891)
Ordained minister in 1849.
Joseph Wutherich (no dates available)
Ordained minister in 1849. Later moved to Hay Township and then to Illinois.
Joseph Ruby (1813-1897)
Ordained: minister in 1852; bishop in 1853.
John Wagler (1820-1908)
Ordained deacon in 1852. Later moved to Indiana (1871). Some of his descendants have recently moved back to Canada with the recent Old Order Amish immigrants.
Joseph Baechler (1817-1891)
Ordained minister in France. Came to Canada in 1852.
Joseph C. Zehr (1822-1915)
Ordained in New York state in 1852. Came to Canada in 1860.
Jacob Bender (1830-1902)
Ordained: deacon in 1871; minister in 1883.
Jacob M. Bender (1830-1914)
Ordained: deacon in 1871; minister in 1883; and bishop in 1887.
Joseph Stiri (1824-1896)
Ordained deacon in New York state. Came to Canada in 1875.

Christian Kropf (1843-1925)
Ordained: deacon in 1889 in Hay Township; minister in East Zorra in 1902.
Michael K. Yantzi (1849-1917)
Ordained: deacon in 1883; minister in 1902; and bishop in 1914.
Joseph Jantzi (1843-1925)
Ordained deacon in Minnesota. Returned to East Zorra in 1910.
Daniel S. Jutzi (1873-19
Ordained: deacon 1902; minister 1914; and bishop in 1917.
Jacob R. Bender (1875-1947)
Ordained minister in 1914.
Peter S. Zehr (1867-1934)
Ordained: deacon in 1919; minister in 1933.
Menno Kipfer (1870-1959)
Ordained: deacon in 1919; minister in 1933.
Daniel Wagler (1897-
Ordained: deacon in 1933, minister 1940.
David Schwartzentruber (1897-)
Ordained: deacon in 1934; minister in 1940.
Joel Schwartzentruber (1891-)
Ordained: deacon in 1940, minister in 1947.
Henry Yantzi (1913-)
Ordained: deacon in 1940; minister in 1947; and bishop in 1948.
Daniel Zehr (1895-)
Ordained deacon in 1947.
Andrew Zehr (189?-19)
Ordained deacon in 1947.

In 1950 all the ministers in East Zorra were stationed with the exception of the bishop, Henry Yantzi. Daniel Wagler and Andrew Zehr (referred to above) served at the 16th Line or East Zorra church. The following ordinations occurred since that time:

Dale Schumm (1932-)
Ordained minister in 1960. Served till 1966 when he left to serve as a missionary in India.
Newton Gingerich (1925-)
Ordained in 1949 in the Mennonite Conference of Ontario. Came to East Zorra in 1966.

4. Blake (1849-1972)

John Oesch (1792-1850)
Ordained in Wilmot. Founded congregation in 1849.
Joseph Wutherich (no dates available)
Ordained in East Zorra 1849. Moved to Blake and later to Illinois.
John Egli (no dates available)
Ordained in Blake. Later moved to Illinois.
Christian Schantz (no dates available)
Ordained deacon. Served till some time after 1885.
Daniel Oesch (no dates available)
Ordained in Blake, son of bishop John Oesch.
John D. Bender (no dates available)
Ordained in Blake, but with Oesch above came under church censure and left church.
John Gascho (1838-1919)
Ordained minister in 1876. Joined the Mennonite church in 1908.

Christian Baechler (1827-1918)
Ordained minister in 1876.
Jacob Gingerich (1833-1890)
Ordained deacon in the 1870s. No exact date available.
Christian Kropf (1843-1925)
Ordained deacon in 1889. Later moved to East Zorra.
Christian Schwartzentruber (1843-1919)
Ordained in Blake (no dates available)
John Gerber (1865-1928)
Ordained deacon in 1916.
Valentine Gerber (1853-1928)
Ordained in Nebraska. Also lived in Minnesota, then back to several different congregations in Ontario.
Solomon Baechler (1884-19
Ordained: deacon in 1928; minister 1940.
Ephraim Gingerich (1917-)
Ordained: minister 1947; bishop 1952. Also served Mennonite congregation in Zurich after 1966. Resigned in 1970.
Cyril Gingerich (1922-)
Ordained: deacon in Zurich Mennonite Congregation in 1946; minister 1951. Served as missionary to Africa till 1969. Then as interim pastor of both Zurich and Blake.
Clayton Kuepfer (1940)
Licensed in 1972 as pastor of Zurich and Blake congregations.

5. Wellesley (Mapleview)
John Jantzi (1806-1881)
Ordained in New York state. Came to Canada 1835. Became bishop in 1859 when congregation was first organized.
John Gerber (1809-1888)
Ordained deacon in 1859.
John Jausie (1815-1875)
Ordained minister in 1854.
Christian Gascho (1838-1872)
Ordained: minister 1865; bishop in 1870.
Joseph L. Lichti (1824-1890)
Ordained minister some time before 1859.
Jacob Wagler (1839-1901)
Ordained: minister in 1873; bishop in 1878.
Christian B. Zehr (1841-1928)
Ordained: deacon 1873; minister 1875; bishop 1914.
Joseph G. Jantzi (1835-1918) (Went with Old Order in 1896)
Ordained deacon in 1865.
Jacob F. Lichti (1866-1944)
Ordained: deacon 1891; minister 1898; bishop 1901.
John Gascho (1864-1949)
Ordained: deacon in 1898; minister in 1913.
Daniel Lebold (1874-1941)
Ordained: deacon 1914; minister 1920; bishop 1926.
Daniel Streicher (1868-1922)
Ordained deacon in 1914.
David Lichti (1870-1937)
Ordained deacon in 1923.
John Wagler (1879-1970)
Ordained deacon in 1923.

Samuel Schultz (1883-1966)
Ordained: minister 1938, bishop 1941.
Samuel Leis (1891-1963)
Ordained minister in 1938.
Samuel Erb (1897-1950)
Ordained minister in 1944.
Christian Streicher (1895-)
Ordained: deacon 1944; minister 1952; bishop 1956.
Christian Erb (1900-1971)
Ordained: deacon 1952; minister 1960; bishop 1967.
Allan Y. Bender (1899-1972)
Ordained minister in 1952.
Alvin Leis (1913-)
Ordained: deacon in 1960; minister in 1966.
Stevanus Gerber (1918-)
Ordained: deacon in 1960; minister in 1966.
Ervin Erb (1917-)
Ordained deacon in 1967.
Jacob Roes (1936-)
Ordained deacon in 1967.

6. Mornington (Poole) (1874-1972)
Joseph Gerber (1838-1910)
Ordained: minister in 1865; bishop 1875. Moved to U.S.A. 1893.
Joseph U. Ropp (1835-1910)
Ordained minister in 1873.
John Kuepfer (1842-1925)
Ordained deacon in 1873.
Christian L. Kuepfer (1839-1916)
Ordained: minister 1879, bishop 1891. Went with Old Order group in 1886.
Andrew Kuepfer (1838-1923)
Ordained minister in 1879. Also joined Old Order in 1886.
Solomon Kuepfer (1853-1934)
Ordained: deacon 1879; minister 1911. Went with Old Order in 1886.
Nicholas Nafziger (1866-1944)
Ordained: minister 1891; bishop 1896. Became bishop of Nafziger congregation 1903.
Peter Spenler (1858-1935)
Ordained minister in 1891. Joined Nafziger group 1903.
John Albrecht (1861-1944)
Ordained: deacon in 1891; minister in 1911. Joined Nafziger group 1903.
John Nafziger (1856-1910)
Ordained minister in 1892. Joined Nafziger group 1903.
Peter Boshart (1870-1942)
Ordained minister in 1903. Transferred membership to Wilmot congregation in 1927.
Christian Schultz (1869-1952)
Ordained: minister 1905; bishop in 1926.
Christian Brunk (1894-1972)
Ordained deacon in 1921. Served over 50 years.
Christian Lichti (
Ordained minister in 1940. Left the congregation in 1959 to join Conservative Mennonites.

Amos Brunk (1893-)
Ordained minister in 1940.
Herbert Schultz (1935-)
Ordained minister in 1955. Resigned in 1970 to complete theological training. Now serving Wanner Mennonite congregation.
Amsey Martin (1929-)
Ordained in 1958 by Ontario Mennonite Conference. Installed pastor of Poole 1970.

7. Cassel (1935-1972)

Ministers from the East Zorra congregation served here until 1950 when Joel Schwartzentruber was stationed as minister and Daniel Zehr as deacon. One ordination has occurred since that time.

Vernon Zehr (1920-)
Ordained minister 1958.

8. Tavistock (1942-1972)

Congregation served by ministers from East Zorra till 1950. Following this David Schwartzentruber was stationed here. Serving since that time have been the following:

Peter Erb (1943-)
Licensed and served for one year 1966-7.
Wilmer Martin (1939-)
Ordained minister in Pennsylvania. Assumed pastorate here in 1968.

9. Riverdale (Millbank) 1946-1972

Begun as a mission in 1946, organized as a separate congregation in 1947. The following men have been ordained here:

Menno Zehr (1903-)
Ordained minister 1948.
Valentine Nafziger (1904-)
Ordained: deacon 1949; bishop 1951.
David Jantzi (1916-)
Ordained minister 1958.

10. Nairn (Ailsa Craig) (1948-1972)

Wilfred Schlegel (1910-)
Ordained minister in 1949.
Daniel Zehr (1935-)
Ordained 1962 as minister. Served congregation until 1965.

A number of young men have assisted in the ministry here. They include:

Kenneth Schwartzentruber, Melvin Otterbein, Myron Ebersol, Jim Helmuth, and John Brubacher.

11. Crosshill (1949-1972)

Begun as a branch of the Mapleview congregation it was served by ministers from that church until 1967 when Stevanus Gerber was stationed here as minister and Ervin Erb as deacon. Both continue to serve in that capacity.

12. Avon (Stratford) (1952-1972)

Begun as a mission with Floyd Baechler as superintendent. Serving first as lay then as a licensed minister was Jacob Spenler till 1962. Ordained at Avon were the following:

Kenneth Bender (1935-)
Licensed 1962, Ordained minister in 1964. Served till 1966. Since then a minister at large in the Conference.
Winston Martin (1939-)
Licensed 1968, Ordained 1970.

13. Valleyview (London) (1953-1972)

Started as a mission with Alvin N. Roth serving as pastor. The following ordinations have taken place:

Alvin N. Roth (1913-)

Licensed 1952, Ordained 1955. No pastoral responsibility here since 1961. Continues as Director of London Mission Services.

Ralph Lebold (1934-)

Licensed 1961. Ordained 1962 as minister.

Walter Friesen

Served as licensed minister for one year.

Glen Horst (1946-)

Commissioned as Associate Minister 1970.

14. Zion (Wellesley) (1953-1972)

Organized as a mission in 1952 it continues under Solomon Bast as a lay minister.

15. Hillcrest (1964-1972)

Organized as an additional congregation with members from the East Zorra church. Henry Yantzi (see under East Zorra) serves as pastor.

16. Bethel Chapel (Parkhill) (1964-1972)

Begun as an Inter-Mennonite congregation it has been served by the following leaders:

John Brubacher (1935)

Licensed 1964. Ordained 1966. Served here till 1969.

Leonard Epp (1930-)

Ordained in the General Conference Mennonite Church. Assumed pastorate here in 1970.

Old Order Congregations

1. Wellesley-Mornington (1888-1891)

Following the division occasioned by the building of meeting houses deacon Joseph G. Jantzi from Wellesley and ministers Christian L. and Andrew Kuepfer plus deacon Solomon Kuepfer became the leaders of the first Old Order congregation in Canada.

2. In 1891 bishops from Holmes County, Ohio helped to organize the Old Order Amish in Wellesley and Mornington Townships into two separate congregations. Additional ordinations in each congregation follow:

Mornington (1891-1972)

Christian L. Kuepfer (1839-1916)

Ordained bishop in 1891. Also served the Wellesley Old Order congregations till 1902.

Solomon Kuepfer (1853-1934)

Ordained minister in 1911.

John Kuepfer (1865-1946)

Ordained: minister 1897; bishop 1913.

Joseph Z. Kuepfer (1881-1967)

Ordained: deacon in 1911; minister 1943.

Jonathan Kuepfer (1869-1955)

Ordained minister in 1916.

Henry S. Albrecht (1870-1951)

Ordained: minister 1924, bishop 1934.

Daniel Steckley (1893-1958)

Ordained minister in 1931.

Christian S. Kuepfer (1895-1934)
Ordained deacon in 1931.
Christian W. Kuepfer (1894-1971)
Ordained deacon in 1945.
Solomon Kuepfer (1896-)
Ordained: deacon 1943, minister 1945, and bishop in 1949.
Gideon Streicher (1916-)
Ordained minister in 1947.
Harvey Jantzi (1925-)
Ordained minister in 1963.
Clarence Kuepfer (1935-)
Ordained: minister 1966, bishop 1969.
Harvey Albrecht (1922-)
Ordained deacon in 1966.

In 1945 there was a division in the Old Order congregations resulting in a new congregation usually referred to as the Steckley District. Ordained to serve this congregation were the following:
Samuel Steckley (1903-)
Ordained: minister 1945; bishop 1946.
Aaron J. Kuepfer (1917-)
Ordained minister in 1953.
William Carter (1920-)
Ordained: minister 1959; bishop 1964.
Menno J. Kipfer (1910-)
Ordained deacon in 1945.
Kenneth Kuepfer (1942-)
Ordained minister in 1968.

In 1969 the original Old Order congregation in Mornington Township was divided into two districts. The new congregation is known as the Upper West District and is served by the following leaders:
Christian W. Kuepfer (1894-1971)
(same as given above)
Samuel K. Zehr (1938-)
Ordained minister in 1970.
Peter S. Kuepfer (1942-)
Ordained minister in 1970.
Rufus Kuepfer (1934-)
Ordained minister in 1971.

Wellesley (1891-1955)

Joseph G. Jantzi was the only ordained man in the Wellesley congregation who went with the Old Order group in 1886. After becoming a separate congregation in 1891 the following ordinations took place.
Peter Jantzi (1842-1917)
Ordained: minister 1891; bishop 1902.
Menno Lichti (1865-1961)
Ordained minister in 1897.
Daniel S. Jantzi (1871-1952)
Ordained deacon in 1911.
Joseph W. Kuepfer (1867-1948)
Ordained: minister 1915, bishop 1916.
Daniel G. Kuepfer (1877-1944)
Ordained: minister 1917; bishop 1942.

Joseph Nafziger (1868-1947)
Ordained deacon in 1912 in the Nafziger congregation and later transferred here.
Amos Z. Albrecht (1904-)
Ordained: minister 1939; bishop 1945.
Joseph K. Jantzi (1912-)
Ordained: minister in 1939.
Joseph N. Jantzi (1914-)
Ordained minister in 1948.
Israel Kuepfer (1922-)
Ordained deacon in 1952.

In 1955 this congregation was divided into two districts. In the Northeast District Amos Z. Albrecht continued as bishop, with the following men ordained since that time:

Eli S. Kuepfer (1916-)
Ordained minister in 1956.
Menno Albrecht (1932-)
Ordained minister in 1961.
David S. Kuepfer (1928-)
Ordained deacon in 1963.

After 1955 the second congregation was known as the Southeast District. Continuing here were Joseph K. and Joseph N. Jantzi as ministers with Israel Kuepfer deacon. Two ordinations have taken place since then.

Joseph K. Jantzi (same as above)
Ordained bishop in 1960.
Samuel K. Jantzi (1914-)
Ordained minister in 1956.

Beachy Amish Congregation

Nafziger (Mornington)

Following the division in the Mornington congregation in 1903 Nicholas Nafziger, Peter Spenler, John Albrecht, and John Nafziger formed what came to be known as the Nafziger congregation. Additional ordinations follow:

John Gerber (1863-1929)
Ordained minister in Michigan. Came here in 1924.
Jacob Wagler (1868-1939)
Ordained deacon in 1912.
Solomon Jantzi (1869-1935)
Ordained in Michigan. Came to Canada in 1928.
Samuel Nafziger (1895-)
Ordained minister in 1933.
Moses Nafziger (1894-1970)
Ordained: minister 1933; bishop 1940.
Valentine Gerber (1853-1928)
Ordained in Nebraska. Also served in Minnesota, Holdimond and Huron Counties in Ontario before joining this congregation.
Jonas Jantzi (1891-1964)
Ordained deacon in 1938.
Joseph J. Steckley (1899-1968)
Ordained minister 1938.
Aaron N. Jantzi (1927-)
Ordained deacon 1968.

Lorne Schmidt (1918-)
Ordained minister 1968.
Leonard Jantzi (1929-)
Ordained minister 1970.
Melvin Roes (1944-)
Ordained minister 1970.

Beachy Amish Congregations

Cedar Grove (Wellesley) (1911-1972)

After the division of 1911 in the Wellesley church bishop Jacob F. Lichti and deacon John Gascho became the initial leaders of the new Lichti or Cedar Grove congregation. Below are listed additional ordinations.

John Gascho was ordained minister in 1913.
David Wagler (1878-1970)
Ordained deacon in 1913.
John Gerber (1872-1948)
Ordained minister in 1916.
Joseph R. Gerber (1875-1958)
Ordained deacon in 1916.
Samuel Lichti (1902-1968) (son of bishop Jacob Lichti)
Ordained in Ohio and returned to Ontario in 1939 and served here till his death in 1968.
Samuel Roth (1895-)
Ordained: minister in 1945; bishop in 1953.
Noah W. Gerber (1906-)
Ordained minister in 1945.
Melvin Jantzi (1933-)
Ordained minister in 1963.
John L. Zehr (1919-)
Ordained deacon in 1963.
Amos Wagler (1899-1945)
Ordained minister in 1941.

Conservative Mennonite Congregation

Bethel (Millbank) (1956-1972)

Organized as a congregation following a division in the Riverdale congregation in 1956. Bishop Valentine Nafziger led the congregation from the beginning. The following ordinations have taken place since that time.

Kenneth Brenneman (1930-)
Ordained: minister 1957; bishop 1972.
Ralph Gerber (1926-)
Ordained deacon in 1962.
Orval Baer (1927-)
Ordained minister in 1971.

Salem Fellowship (1969-1972)

Organized in 1969 by families from the Cedar Grove and Nafziger congregations by bishop Allen Slabauch of Napanee, Indiana who continues to have bishop oversight of the congregation. Ordained to serve as ministers were the following:

Lorne Steckley (1933-)
Ordained minister in 1969.
Mervin L. Kuepfer (1942-)
Ordained deacon in 1970.

Maple Grove (1969-1972)

Formed by a group who left the East Zorra congregation under the leadership of minister Daniel Wagler. The following ordinations have taken place:

Oliver Yantzi (1918-)

Ordained minister in 1969.

Maurice Witzel (1928-)

Ordained minister in 1969.

Milverton Conservative Fellowship (1970-1972)

Organized after a division in the Bethel congregation (see above) in 1970. Ralph Gerber, deacon, was the only ordained man in the group that left Bethel. The following ordinations have taken place since then:

David Fischer (1941-)

Ordained minister in 1970.

Daniel Gascho (1940-)

Ordained minister in 1970.

Constitution of the Ontario Amish Mennonite Conference

Adopted June 16th, 1925
at the East Zorra A.M. Meeting House
Near Tavistock, Ont.

Article I.

Name

This conference shall be known as the Ontario Amish Mennonite Conference.

Article II.

Object

The object of this Conference shall be to consider questions relative to the work of the church, and adopt such measures as shall advance the cause of Christ, and promote the unity and general welfare of the church.

Article III.

Membership

1. Elders (Bishops) ministers and deacons are members of this conference.

2. Where churches are not supplied with ministers this conference recommends that one delegate be sent to conference for each 100 members or fraction thereof, who, with their letter of recommendation shall be members.

3. Churches having ministers who for some providential cause can not attend, may send delegates from their brethren, equal to their number of ministers and deacons, as members.

4. Each member shall be entitled to one vote.

Article IV.

Officers

1. The officers of this Conference shall consist of a Moderator, Assistant Moderator, Secretary and Assistant Secretary, and Treasurer.

2. The officers shall be elected by the conference for one year, or until their successors are elected or appointed, except the Treasurer.

3. The officers of this Conference shall constitute the Executive Committee, which shall have the general supervision of the Conference work, shall appoint time and place of holding Conference and fill vacancies in any office until the next regular meeting of Conference.

Article V.

Duties of Offices

1. The Moderator shall preside over the Conference when in session, and perform all duties specified or implied in this Constitution pertaining to his office.

2. The Assistant Moderator shall, in the absence of the Moderator or by his appointment, act as Moderator.

3. The Secretary shall keep an accurate record of the proceedings of this Conference and shall read the same at the next regular meeting. After its approval he shall enter his report in a conference record book before he is released from office, and shall perform such other duties as usually pertain to his office.

4. The Treasurer shall solicit and receive funds from the several congregations of this Conference, necessary to defray the expenses herein mentioned.

(a) He shall pay the expenses of the ministers who are having charge of the smaller congregations and scattered members not supplied with ministers, whilst he is administering to their spiritual needs.

(b) Other expenses may be paid when ordered so by this Conference.

(c) He shall keep a record of all money received and paid out by him and report the same at each regular Conference meeting.

(d) He shall be elected by the Conference for a term of three years.

Article VI.

Committees

All committees shall be appointed by the Moderator with the approval of Conference, excepting the executive committee and committees on arbitration, which shall be elected by Conference.

Article VII.

Conference Decisions

The adoption of all decisions and resolutions of the Conference shall be determined by a majority of two-thirds of all votes cast.

Article VIII.

Conference Leadership

The Conference shall endeavor to lead and unify the churches in upholding such rules and discipline as are necessary to restrain upon Gospel principles, the great modern tendency to worldliness and in promoting spiritual life in the churches.

Article IX.

Meetings

1. The Conference shall meet annually unless in the judgment of the executive committee there is no special need of a meeting it may be postponed until the following year.
2. Order of Exercises:
   - (a) Devotional Exercises.
   - (b) Reading and Approval of Minutes.
   - (c) Conference Sermon.
   - (d) Testimonies.
   - (e) Consideration of Questions.
   - (f) Reports.
   - (g) Appointment of Committees.
   - (h) Miscellaneous Business.
   - (i) Election of Officers.
   - (j) Adjournment.

Article X.

Amendments

No amendment or alteration shall be made to this Constitution without the concurrence of three-fourths of the members present. Notice of the proposed amendment shall be given to each member of Conference at least thirty days before the meeting at which action shall be taken upon it.

Rules and Discipline of the ONTARIO AMISH MENNONITE CONFERENCE

Adopted Feb. 2, 1926, at the Wellesley A.M. meeting house, near Wellesley, Ont.

I. Faith

1. We are orthodox in our belief, we accept all of the Holy Scriptures as inspired, therefore the only true and infallible guide. John 8:31. II. Tim. 3:16-17. I. Pet. 1:25. Luke 21:33.

2. We believe in God the Creator; Christ the Redeemer, and the Holy Spirit as our Guide, Teacher and Comforter. Gen. 1. Acts 4:11-12. John 16:13; 14:26.

3. We confess and believe that Jesus Christ and His Apostles recognized and established a visible church with due authority built upon the true foundation Christ being the chief corner stone. Matth. 16:18; 18:17-18. Eph. 2:19-22. Heb. 10:25.

II. Calling the Ministry or Ordination

Sec. 1. The ministers and deacons shall be chosen from the brotherhood by the voice of the church. If more than the required number of candidates are voted for by the church, the lot shall be used to decide whom the Lord has chosen Acts 1:15-23; 6:1-6 such person shall be ordained by bishops. Titus 1:5.

Sec. 2. The bishops or elders shall be chosen from among the ministers by the voice of the congregation where they are to officiate. If the congregation fails to be unanimous in their choice of a candidate it shall be decided by lot as to who shall be ordained. Acts 1:15-23; 14:23.

Sec. 3. Candidates for bishops, ministers and deacons shall be examined regarding their faith and their forms of doctrine upheld by the church giving special attention to the qualifications found in I. Tim. 3:1-13. Tit. 1:5-9. No one shall be ordained or even taken into the lot who does not have at least to a reasonable degree these qualifications. However no one shall be ordained bishop (elder), minister or deacon without the consent of Conference and of the congregation where he is to serve.

Duties of Ministry

Sec. 1. It is the duty of the bishop in addition to the ordinary work of the ministry to instruct, baptize and to receive into church fellowship penitent believers, to officiate at communion and feet-washing services, to solemnize marriages, to excommunicate (with the consent of the church) the disobedient and to have the general oversight of the church. Matth. 28:19. Luke 22:19-20. John 13:1-17. I Cor. 5:13. I Pet. 5:1-3.

Sec. 2. It is the duty of the minister to preach the Word, to instruct applicants for church membership and to look after the general welfare of the church. I Cor. 1:17. II. Tim. 4:1-5.

Sec. 3. It is the duty of the deacon to receive and hold funds given for charitable purposes, to distribute them among the needy, to keep an accurate record of all such receipts and disbursements, said records to be always open to any member of the church for examination. He shall seek to bring about reconciliation between members when discord prevails, to visit transgressors and admonish them to repent and when unsuccessful shall report to the Bishop in charge. He shall assist in the administration of the ordinances and when given due notice by the minister or Bishop perform the duties of minister. Acts 6:1-10. I. Tim. 4:14-16.

Sec. 4. Relieving from Duty — When a bishop, minister or deacon has proven himself unworthy, unqualified or incapable of performing the duties of his office he may be relieved from such by the counsel and consent of the Conference and church.

III. Water Baptism.

We believe water baptism to be the initiatory rite into the visible church and should be administered to all true believers. Since the Holy Spirit baptism was called a baptism by the Saviour, which was by pouring, we believe it to be in perfect harmony with the Bible that water baptism should be by pouring. Acts 1:5; 2:17, 18, 41. Matth. 28:19; 3:13-17.

IV. Communion

Instituted by Christ, taught and practiced by His Apostles. The partaking of the bread and fruit of the vine is a memorial of the broken body and shed blood of Jesus Christ. As a body of believers having a unity of faith in the bonds of peace and love should frequently be observed to keep the suffering and death of our Lord vividly before our minds. Matth. 26:26-27. Luke 22:19-20. I. Cor. 11:23-26. Acts 2:42. I. Cor. 10:16-21. I. Cor. 12:12-13.

V. Washing Saints' Feet

We believe in washing of the saints' feet as taught and practiced by our Lord and His followers. A true symbol of humility. John 13:4-17. II. Tim. 5:10. Matth. 28:20. Luke 22: 17.

VI. Devotional Covering

According to the inspired Word it is required that all women professing godliness wear a special devotional head covering during worship (or engaged in teaching, prayer or prophecying) and for the same reason it is required that men have their heads uncovered during worship. I. Cor. 11:1-5; verses 14 and 15 refer to the natural covering whilst the preceding verses refer to an artificial covering or veiling according to the new version. II. Thess. 2:15; 3:6.

VII. Salutation

Salutation with the holy kiss a symbol of Christian love and commanded in God's Word. Rom. 16:16. I. Pet. 5:14. I. Thess. 5:26.

VIII. Anointing With Oil

Taught by James 5:14, 15, 16. A symbol of God's grace manifested in healing power.

(a) Should be exercised in cases of extreme illness.

(b) Should be accompanied with full faith, for the prayer of faith shall save the sick.

(c) Should not be considered an unction for the soul to be administered in dying moments.

IX. Marriage

That marriage was divinely instituted for the propagation, purity and happiness of the human race; that it receives divine sanction between one man and one woman only; that the bond is dissoluble only by death (divorces forbidden by Scipture, Matth. 19:6,9); that there should be no marriage between a believer and an unbeliever, nor between members of different denominations. Gen. 2:18. Mark 10:12-13. Rom. 7:2.

X. Obligations to Government

We regard our obligations to the government binding so long as it does not conflict with the teaching of Christ and His Apostles, and should often remember those in authority in prayer. Rom. 13:1-8. Tit. 3:1-2. Matth. 22:21. Acts 4: 19-20. John 18:37. I. Tim. 2:1-2.

XI. Nonconformity to the World

(a) Intemperance. Prov. 23:29-35. Gal. 5:21. I. Cor. 9:25. I. Pet. 4:3.

(b) Unholy Conversation. Eph. 4:29. I. Tim. 2:16.

(c) Fashionable Attire. I. Tim. 2:9. I. Peter 3:3. Jer. 4:30.

(d) Covetousness. Col. 3:5. I. Tim. 6:10-11.

(e) Worldly Amusements. Titus 2:12. I. Pet. 4:3-4.

(f) Sunday Desecration. Gen. 2:3. Exod. 20:8.

(g) Pride. James 4:6. I. Peter 5:5.

XII. Nonresistance

We are opposed to carnal warfare because Christ and His Apostles taught a defenseless doctrine both by precept and example. Matth. 5:38-45; 26:51-52. Luke 9:51-57. II. Cor. 10:4. Rom. 12:19-21.

XIII. Nonswearing of Oaths

Since we have covenanted with God our words shall be yea, yea, nay, nay, whatsoever more is cometh from the evil. Matth. 5:33-37. James 5:12.

XIV. Secret Societies.

They are wrong because they are generally oath bound, are unequally yoked with the unbeliever, are detrimental to Christian churches and antagonistic to spirit of Christ. II. Corinthians 6:14-17. Heb. 10:25. Eph. 5:11-12. John 18:20. John 3:19-21.

XV. Life Insurance

Life insurance is wrong because it makes merchandise of human lives. II. Peter 2:3. I Tim. 6:9-11-17.

XVI. Mission Work

We encourage mission work and a liberal support to home and foreign missions from each congregation in this Conference district. Matth. 28:19-20. Acts 1:8. II. Cor. 9:6-7. Gal. 6:9.

XVII. Conclusion

We consider it the duty of every member of this Conference to be present at each Conference and also urge the laity to attend. Rom. 12:11. Heb. 10:25.

Plan of Salvation

The plan of salvation implies:

(1) A recognition of God as the Creator and preserver of all things.

(2) That man created perfect and in the image of his Maker through the transgression of our first parents, fell.

(3) That in consequence of this fall, became alienated from God.

(4) That God and man became reconciled through the shedding of the blood of our Lord Jesus Christ.

(5) That salvation is now offered as a free gift to all them that accept the terms of the Gospel principles that primarily affect all believers, viz:

(a) Faith. Heb. 11:1,6. "Now Faith is the substance of things hoped for, the evidence of things not seen." But without faith it is impossible to please Him, for he that cometh to God must believe that He is, and that He is a rewarder of them that diligently seek Him.

(b) Repentance. Acts 17:30. II. Cor. 7:10. And the times of this ignorance God winked at; but now God commandeth all men everywhere to repent. For godly sorrow worketh repentance to salvation not to be repented of: but the sorrow of the world worketh death.

(c) Conversion. Matth. 18:3. Verily, I say unto you, except ye be converted, and become as little children, ye shall not enter into the kingdom of heaven.

(d) Regeneration. John 3:3. Verily, Verily, I say unto thee except a man be born again, he can not see the Kingdom of God.

(e) Justification. Rom. 3:28. James 2:20. Heb. 10:38. "Therefore we conclude that a man is justified by faith without the deeds of the law." "But wilt thou know, O vain man, that faith without works is dead." "Now the just shall live by faith, but if any man draw back, my soul shall have no pleasure in him."

(f) Redemption. John 3:16. For God so loved the world that he gave His only begotten Son, that whosoever believeth in Him should not perish but have everlasting life.

(g) Sanctification. John 17:19. And for their sakes I sanctify myself that they also might be sanctified through the truth.

DANIEL S. JUTZI,
Moderator.
DANIEL H. STEINMANN,
Assist. Moderator.
CHR. R. BRUNK,
Secretary.
JACOB R. BENDER,
Assist. Secretary.
PETER S. ZEHR,
Treasurer.

Western Ontario Mennonite Conference

Statements as revised and accepted, June 1970

Constitution

Presented to delegates of Western Ontario Mennonite Conference at annual sessions, June 1970.

Title: Constitution of the Western Ontario Mennonite Conference Incorporated.

Preamble: Whereas it is essential and in the best interest of the church that she have proper guidance in her assemblies and in the operation of her affairs the following articles of Constitution are presented.

1. **Name**
   Western Ontario Mennonite Conference Incorporated.
2. **Purpose**
   The purpose of this conference shall be:
   (a) to provide opportunity for members of the conference to relate together in Christian fellowship.
   (b) to consider questions relative to the work of the church:
      1. as she seeks to fulfill her mission in the world.
      2. as she seeks to function effectively as a Christian organization.
   (c) to provide opportunity for its various congregations to unify their efforts in performing tasks too large for individual congregations.
   (d) to assist its various congregations in fulfilling their tasks of nurture and outreach.
   (e) to provide a channel to relate to the larger Mennonite brotherhood and other Christian groups.
3. **Voting Delegates**
   (a) All ordained, licensed and appointed persons.
   (b) The following persons from each congregation:
      1. Mission Board representative
      2. Christian Nurture representative
      3. Youth representative
      4. Congregational treasurer
   (c) Congregations with a membership of over 200 shall appoint one additional person.
   (d) All conference appointees.
   (e) 20 voting delegates present shall constitute a quorum.

4. **Executive Committee**

(a) The executive committee of this conference shall consist of moderator, assistant moderator, secretary, ministerial superintendent, mission board representative (chairman), Christian nurture representative (chairman), youth representative (president).

(b) Term of office:
Moderator, assistant moderator, secretary, treasurer, and ministerial superintendent shall serve for a period of three years. No officer shall succeed himself more than once. All other executive committee members shall serve by virtue of office in their respective committees.

(c) Duties of officers:

1. The moderator shall call and preside at all meetings of the executive and delegate body.
2. The assistant moderator shall act as required by the absence of the moderator or at his request.
3. The secretary shall keep an accurate record of the proceedings of this conference and shall submit the same for approval at the next regular meeting whereupon they shall be entered in the conference record book. He shall be custodian of all conference records and shall pass the same on to the succeeding secretary. The secretary shall at the request of the moderator send notices of meetings, business to be discussed, etc.
4. The treasurer shall be custodian of all conference funds, and shall pay expenses as agreed upon by the executive committee and delegate body. He shall be responsible to prepare an annual financial statement.

5. **Organization.**

The church, through the conference, recognizes existing boards and committees serving the conference, and may appoint other committees as may be decided upon in light of current needs. Committees appointed for specific tasks shall terminate upon completing their assignment. — See appendix for duties of standing conference committees.

6. **Authority of Conference**

(a) The conference shall have the oversight of, and restrictive power over, all organizations, committees, etc., of any kind, which have originated, or shall originate under, or by the consent of, the conference.

(b) Relative to problems arising in local congregations, the conference shall be responsible to give assistance or advice at the request of the congregations involved, or at the discretion of the executive committee.

7 **Meetings**

(a) This conference shall meet once each year at such time and place as shall be designated by the conference, for inspiration, fellowship, business and reorganization.

(b) All other meetings of conference shall be called by the moderator in consultation with the executive committee.

(c) The secretary shall give advance notice in writing of any conference body meeting to be held between regular sessions and include in the notice the agenda for the proposed meetings.

8. **Ministry**

The conference recognizes that there is a scriptural basis for congregational organization as given in the New Testament. We believe this leadership ought to be shared by both ordained and lay brethren. Each congregation shall therefore ordain, license and/or appoint qualified and gifted persons to meet the spiritual needs of its members. For more specific instructions see appendix.

9. **Resolutions and Conference Decisions**

(a) After a decision or resolution is reached either by consensus or majority vote the delegates of each congregation shall make application in line with the suggested resolution or decision in their respective congregations. All decisions and resolutions shall become as an ideal toward which to strive.

10. **Amendments**

(a) Notice of the proposed amendment shall be given to each delegate of conference at least thirty days before the meeting at which action is to be taken.

(b) No amendments shall be made to this constitution without the concurrence of two-thirds of the delegates present.

(c) Upon consensus of those present, an amendment may be made at any given meeting without prior notice.

Purpose of Standing Conference Committees
Christian Nurture Council

The purpose of this organization shall be to promote, give assistance and guidance to local congregations in the area of Christian work and nurture, to give opportunity for the discussion of mutual problems relating to the growth and development of mature Christian persons, and to strengthen the faith, unity and fellowship of the brotherhood.

The Purpose & Philosophy of the Western Ontario Mennonite Mission Board

1. The Board serves as an interpreter of the church's larger mission program and seeks to develop a sense of responsibility for mission in the local communities and around the world.
2. The Board seeks to stimulate mission giving and is a channel for mission funds. The treasurer handles funds from the churches, channeling them to Elkhart or to Social projects. The Capital Investment fund provides a capital resource for developing churches and other types of outreach. The Student Aid fund is administered by the Board as well. The Evangel has been funded through the Board Treasury in cooperation with the Ontario Conference.
3. The Board assists congregations in developing projects which would be difficult to handle alone (e.g. the London Rescue Mission) and aids in the development of emerging congregations. It also explores possible new areas of outreach (e.g. Bookrack Evangelism).
4. There is involvement in the inter-Mennonite Board both financially and through the representation of one member from the executive as well as one member from the conference executive.

Purpose of Stewardship & Finance Committee

A. To promote Christian Stewardship, meaning that under the Lordship of Christ this involves our time, talent and material blessings.

B. To present a Proposed Giving Guide, to draw our attention to the needs of the different organizations that we as a conference support.

C. To serve as a counselling body in the area of finances and giving, both to the conference and congregations.

Appendix on the Ministry

I Ordination

A. We recognize our traditional threefold ordained ministry (bishop, minister and deacon) as not in violation of scripture although not the precise New Testament pattern. Those congregations wishing to continue this pattern shall have the privilege of so doing.

We suggest a more practical pattern for our congregations might be to limit ordination to one pastor, or pastor and assistant pastor in larger congregations, and that the congregation license or appoint additional lay members to assist in the ministry.

We also recognize that there is no magical power in the term or ceremony of ordination. Any congregation may therefore simply appoint or commission any person to be its pastor, with all the rights and privileges of an ordained minister, taking into consideration the scriptural qualifications of such a person.

II Licensing

A. The Conference may license a brother to preach the gospel and perform the duties of a pastor, except performing marriages, baptismal service, or serve communion alone.

1. All persons considered for licensing shall meet the same scriptural standards as ordained ministers.
2. Shall be licensed for one year at a time, and the total probationary period shall not exceed three years.
3. After each year period the executive committee shall study and evaluate every licensed brother's work and bring a recommendation to conference before re-appointment.
4. All licensed brethren shall have the privilege of attending all conference meetings and have voting rights.

III Lay Ministers

A. Appointment

A congregation may appoint a person or persons as a lay minister to assist the pastor in his ministry to the congregation. It is suggested that this be a three year appointment with a mutual assessment by the congregation at the end of each term.

B. Duties

A lay minister should perform any or all ministerial duties requested by the pastor and/or the congregation except for those responsibilities specifically assigned to the ordained ministry.

IV **Conference Minister**

A. Appointment

The executive committee of conference shall appoint a man for the position of conference minister from among the ministers of the conference body, to serve for a period of three years, not succeeding himself more than once.

B. Duties

1. As indicated previously the conference minister would be a pastor to all ministers in the conference and as such should have the total welfare of each minister at heart.
2. It is his responsibility to assist all ministers, and ministerial committees to designate and share responsibilities in the congregation so as to make the most efficient use of the talents and gifts God has bestowed for the edification of the body of Christ.
3. The Conference minister should seek to evaluate each minister's work, give helpful counsel and share any spiritual concerns he may have, ever seeking to help each minister to become a better pastor.
4. He would be a negotiator between ministers and congregations, pastor and ministerial committee; and between pastor, ministers, ministerial committees, and the conference body.

C. Remuneration

The finance committee in consultation with the executive committee shall review whatever figure is arrived at yearly and make necessary adjustments.

V **Ministerial Support**

While the conference does not necessarily recommend a fully paid one man ministry it is conscious that the Lord ordained that they which preach the gospel should live of the gospel, Matt. 10: 9, 10 I Cor. 9: 13, 14. It is also evident that the early church did not interpret this ordinance legalistically, but was quite flexible. Nevertheless, the Apostles recognized the need for additional ministerial helpers in order that they might give their time fully to the ministry of the Word and prayer, Acts 6:1-4. We believe this is just as necessary today as it was then and that each congregation ought to seriously consider its responsibility in this area, and should probably have at least one supported minister in order that he may give adequate time and attention to the spiritual needs of the congregation. It is envisioned that the Conference Minister would work with each congregation on this matter.

VI **Ministerial Change**

A. We are not necessarily advocating departure from our traditional pattern of having a minister serve only one congregation in his life-time. On the other hand, we recognize that a minister may be able to make a greater contribution to the brotherhood by changing pastorates. We further believe that a change of ministers may at times be to the spiritual benefit of our congregations. While no term of service is suggested in any specific number of years, we would caution against too frequent change, or having the desire for change become a mere escape by either pastor or congregations from facing responsibilities or difficulties.

B. Any minister or congregation desiring a change should follow the following pattern:
   1. Discuss such a desire with the Conference Minister before making such a desire public knowledge.
   2. Have sucn change approved by the Conference Minister and the Executive committee of conference.

VII **Ministers Without Duty**

A. Retirement:

We believe a minister should serve as long as he is able. However, we would deem it advisable that a minister or bishop lay down administrative duties and responsibilities and serve only in an unofficial capacity after he reaches a certain age. The particular age this should be done would depend on a number of factors and cannot be spelled out precisely but might be anywhere from 65-75.

B. Ministers Without Congregational Responsibility:
   1. If for circumstantial, or any other reasons a minister changes his membership to another congregation, he shall not assume a ministerial role unless specifically requested by that congregation.
   2. A minister without congregational responsibility may be appointed as a minister at large in the conference at his request and the discretion of conference.
   3. Any minister who no longer relates to the Mennonite Church either in the congregational, or service level shall forfeit his ministerial status.

VIII Procedure for Processing Ministerial Candidates, Western Ontario Mennonite Conference.
— Copies in Conference file for use at discretion of Conference Minister.

Conference Discipline

The Western Ontario Mennonite Conference in session at Steinman Mennonite Church on January 18, 1969 assigned the Conference Executive the responsibility of writing a Conference Discipline as a guide for our congregations. Upon careful consideration of the assignment and after discussion of the theme at the 1969 June Conference sessions and hearing the recommendations of the listening committee and receiving counsel from various congregations, we, the executive, present the following statement for your consideration.

We believe that discipline is a necessary exercise for the Christian, and that it finds its best expression in a voluntary self-discipline practised by the mature believer in joyful obedience to the Lordship of Christ and Christian principles. We recognize, however, that as brethren, we are interdependent needing each other's guidance, counsel, and support.

We believe that the times in which we live provide a tremendous challenge to the Christian church to demonstrate genuine brotherhood in the midst of diversity, personal responsibility in a permissive society, and a Christ-like compassion and action in a world of greed and need. This challenge can only be met as individuals, congregations, and denominations practise a voluntary self-discipline which alone can free them to be witnesses to Jesus Christ and the Kingdom He came to inaugurate.

As an aid to accomplish this we submit the following guidelines. —

(1) **The first requirement in discipline is the Word preached and practised.**

We recognize that God is the final authority for all of life, and has revealed His will in the Bible. The Bible however, is a vast and complex collection of writings, and easily lends itself to misinterpretation, II Peter 3:16. II Tim. 2:15. We urge, therefore, that special priority be given to the moral law, (the ten commandments) and to the personal teachings of our Lord Jesus Christ, taking into account how the Prophets and Epistle writers understood and interpreted this central core of Divine Revelation.

It is important that each congregation give continued attention to its God-given responsibility of maintaining a scriptural discipline. Not a legalistic and vain attempt to "control" the brother, but rather a compassionate attempt to "gain" him. Matt. 18:10-15; and furthermore that each congregation face the issues that confront it, and by a process of prayerful searching of the Word, mature and open discussion of the problems, find the answers that "seem good to the Holy Spirit and to us."

(2) **Discipline must be Redemptive.**

Its purpose is not to expose the sinner, to subject him to shame or embarrassment, I Peter 4:8, nor is it intended to punish or despise those who have fallen, Matt. 18:11-14.

If however, the sinner, in spite of the warnings of the Holy Spirit, the exhortations of Christian friends, the compassionate concern of the Church, goes on to rejection of the Christian faith and fellowship in the Brotherhood, it becomes the painful duty of the congregation to excommunicate him or her. Hopefully this will destroy any false hope of salvation, and will become a step in the process of restoration.

(3) **Disciplinary actions need to involve the entire congregation.**

While this is primarily the responsibility of the congregation, the Conference can and should serve in a counselling and advisory capacity, so that there can be some unification of witness as well as a stabilizing influence on congregations who may be inclined to "do that which is right in their own eyes", and so alienate themselves from the larger body.

The resources of the congregation should be used to win back those who have strayed, Matt. 18:15-17. Only after sincere, and repeated efforts by both ministers and lay members should the congregation acknowledge the severing of relationships.

(4) **Unity without Uniformity.**

There can be concensus in the life of the congregations on basic principles, without having total agreement on the application in everyday life. Because of the wider spread in culture, the widely diverse occupational employment and interest, the divisive religious influences to which people are subjected via radio and television, we again have problems similar to those encountered by the early Church attempting to bring together Jewish and Gentile Christians. We plead with each congregation to stress acceptance and toleration, such as taught in Rom. 14 and I Cor. chapters 8 to 10, and so avoid the Church divisions which are a disgrace to a church professing nonresistance, and are destroying effective outreach, John 13:55, John 17:21-23.

(5) **We also suggest that the Mennonite Confession of Faith (1963) and, or, the Dordrecht Confession (1632) serve as a guide in faith and practice for our Conference.**

We recognize the value of the broader Denomination emphasis in maintaining the Anabaptist principles and the proven traditions of the Mennonite Church.

Policies on Cooperative Church Extension

Preamble

In view of the emerging congregation in the city of London, the possibility of a united effort between the Amish Mennonite and the Old Mennonite Conferences has been discussed. Present Mennonite interests in the city such as London Rescue Mission, Golden Rule Book Store, the presence of Mennonite families and professional people, and the spiritual ministry to Mennonite students at the University of Western Ontario, would seem to indicate the advisability of combining our resources in church extension.

Following is a suggested outline for the basis of a cooperative effort in church extension.

Spiritual Concerns

1. For the spiritual care of church members from our respective conferences who reside in the city of London temporarily or permanently.
2. For new opportunities to share the gospel.

3. For a unified Mennonite witness in the city of London.

Doctrinal Basis

1. The doctrinal Confession of Faith as subscribed to by both Conference groups.
2. The Constitution as arranged by the emerging church, and approved by the parent bodies.
3. The "Membership Commitment" ascribed to by all applicants for church membership.

Administrative Procedure

1. The emerging church would affiliate with the Conference which initiates the project. If a change should be requested by the local group, this could be done only by mutual consultation with the parent bodies.
2. Persons from Mennonite bodies other than the initiating Conference, would be urged to become associate members of the emerging church.
3. The future establishment of a second congregation in the city shall take place by mutual consent of parent bodies.

Financial Responsibility

1. The initiating Conference shall assume financial responsibility for the project.
2. The other parent body shall be ready to assist by voluntary contributions, loans for building project, etc.
3. Associate members are encouraged to wholeheartedly support the program of the emerging church in every way possible.

Conclusion

These policies have been agreed upon by the Executive Committees of the Amish and Old Mennonite Mission Boards. It is recognized that future experience or circumstances may require reconsideration on any aspect of this agreement. Any changes, however, shall be made by mutual consent.

November 21, 1961

Index